Pacific
Shift

Pacific Shift

William Irwin Thompson

Sierra Club Books · San Francisco

The Sierra Club, founded in 1892 by John Muir, has devoted itself to the study and protection of the earth's scenic and ecological resources—mountains, wetlands, woodlands, wild shores and rivers, deserts and plains. The publishing program of the Sierra Club offers books to the public as a nonprofit educational service in the hope that they may enlarge the public's understanding of the Club's basic concerns. The point of view expressed in each book, however, does not necessarily represent that of the Club. The Sierra Club has some sixty chapters coast to coast, in Canada, Hawaii, and Alaska. For information about how you may participate in its programs to preserve wilderness and the quality of life, please address inquiries to Sierra Club, 730 Polk Street, San Francisco, CA 94109.

LIBRARY OF CONGRESS CATALOGING IN PUBLICATION DATA

Thompson, William Irwin.
Pacific shift.

Includes index.
1. Civilization, Modern—1950–   . 2. East and West.
3. Civilization—Philosophy. I. Title
CB430.T47 1986   901   85-8167
ISBN 0-87156-750-4

Jacket design Copyright © 1986 Lawrence Ratzkin
Book design by Wolfgang Lederer

Printed in the United States of America

10   9   8   7   6   5   4   3   2   1

Dedication

*I would like to dedicate this book to two
of my colleagues in the Lindisfarne Fellowship.
First, to the memory of Gregory Bateson in gratitude
for all that he taught us when he worked on*
Mind and Nature *during his year as Lindisfarne's
scholar in residence. It is my hope that
Gregory would look upon this book as another
step to an ecology of mind. And, second,
to Maurice Strong, the* animateur *of Lindisfarne's
solar village in Colorado. From his work in
setting up the United Nations Environmental Programme
to establishing a solar village at the Baca,
Colorado, Maurice has taken René Dubos's advice of
"thinking globally and acting locally" to heart.
More scientists will have to learn to think
like Gregory, more businessmen to act like Maurice,
if the Pacific is truly to become the shore
of a new Mediterranean for another classical,
but planetary civilization.*

Contents

Appendix
containing color diagrams
follows Index

Acknowledgments

This book was written in Switzerland in 1984 and presented as a series of public lectures and colloquia for the Faculty of Social Science of the University of Hawaii at Manoa in Honolulu. Chapter Three was presented as the Marvin B. Anderson lectures, under the direction of Dean D. Neubaurer, and Chapter Four was given in colloquia for the Social Science Research Institute, under the direction of Professor Donald Topping. I would like to express my gratitude to both Dean Neubauer and Professor Topping for so generously supporting my research and providing me with the time and facilities with which to prepare this book for publication.

I would also like to express my deep gratitude to Professor Manfred Henningsen of the Department of Political Science who was responsible in bringing me to the University of Hawaii, first in 1981, and again in 1985. Professor Henningsen also read the manuscript and helped me in its last stages of correction. Since Professor Henningsen works in Germany as well as Hawaii, his appreciation of the philosophical movements beyond eurocentric thinking is profound, and I am profoundly in his debt.

Politics Unbound:
The World
That's After Us

*P*olitics unbound from the nation-state is the world that's after us, taking hold of our poetic imaginations in this century, but making claim to our political allegiances in the next. No escape except annihilation can protect us from this ancient Greek necessity, for all our efforts to avoid changing only seem to have thrust changes upon us.

It will not be in the rational forms of the Enlightenment that world political leaders will come together in some Planetary Constitutional Convention,[1] for such conscious, volitional activity would require a relaxed openness to the future, and in the late 1970s humanity everywhere willed to reject transformation and reassert a new and more hysterical form of the fundamentalism of the past, from the Islamic fundamentalism of the Shiites to the industrial fundamentalism of the Reaganites. And so humanity has precipitated its collective unconscious into the world as the part of itself it sees as "other" and calls the environment. Of necessity, then, it will be in the form of a globally damaged ecology that the new world body politic will experience itself: not as the legalistic creation of patriarchal states, but as the unconscious manifestation of the planet; not the reactionary involutions of Ouranos that seek to abort all change, but the creative evolution of Gaia that emasculates old gods with new and subtle technologies.[2]

The only head of state who understands this new body politic is the Dalai Lama. At a meeting at the Zen Center in San Francisco in 1979 he told the small group assembled there that: "When man changes the environment too quickly, say, for example, by burning the oceans of oil in the earth's crust and turning them into a gas in the earth's atmosphere, he creates a situation in which the environment then changes at a rate faster than his own rate of adaptation." The Dalai Lama was coming to his knowledge through spiritual rather than scientific means, but his articulation of Buddhist thought was perfectly commensurate with the cybernetics of Gregory Bateson or the Gaia Hypothesis of the atmospheric chemist James Lovelock, and biologist Lynn Margulis. Both Lovelock and Bateson nodded with wide-eyed approval and amazement when later I passed on the Dalai Lama's remarks to them.

This discontinuity between the rate of environmental change and the rate of human adaptation is what can be termed, in the theories of the mathematical topologist René Thom, a "catastrophe,"[3] but to be able to perceive the rate of change we need to step back to consider the history of other changes.

If we draw up a list of the major transformations of natural and cultural history, we involve ourselves in the political act of creating a history, and this act has implicit in it not simply the creation of a new past, but also a new future.

The transformation of history is itself created in the creation of a history of transformations. This came home to me rather informally one morning in 1979 around the breakfast table at Lindisfarne in Manhattan. The biologist Francisco Varela, who was then our scholar-in-residence, the physicist Eric Schwartz, and I were discussing the idea of cultural transformations, and as we drew up a list of the major events of universal history, we noticed that the list seemed to describe a logarithmic progression in the rate of change. It would seem that Henry Adams had been right when he talked about the "acceleration of history."[4] Our "Log of Earth" (see page 5) describes the pattern as we saw it.

Transformations first take billions of years, from the "Big Bang" to the origin of the solar system; but with the emergence of life there is an acceleration, and evolutionary changes begin to take place in millions of years, then in hundreds of thousands. With the emergence of human culture there is a further acceleration, and change begins to manifest in tens of thousands of years. With the emergence of civilization, the rate of change shifts into millennia; then with the emergence of Western science, the rate of change shifts to centuries. Now, with the appearance of microelec-

tronics and genetic engineering, a change that spells a movement from evolution by natural selection to evolution by
cultural intrusion, the rate of change shifts to decades, even
years.

If one continues along the time line, it would indicate
that the "singularity" of the beginning is to be matched by
some sort of singularity at the end, a climax of history that
is already upon us. Certainly, genetic engineering could
mean that the end of history has already happened, and that
now we merely await some great magnification, be it accidental plague or the emergence of scientific supermen, to
allow us to see rather tardily that "the end of man" came
while we all were busy looking in the opposite direction.

Then again, philosophers have been trying to warn us for
some time. From Nietzsche to Heidegger to Foucault,
philosophers have been mumbling something about "the
end of man,"[5] but since life goes on and we still have to get
up and go to work, it is hard to know what to do with
philosophy. Perhaps this acceleration of history is simply an
illusion, a subjective perspective that the observer gives to
history in the act of perceiving it through the selection of
events he or she deems important. Or perhaps consciousness
is itself an acceleration of time that can only see those events
that are cotemporal with itself, and, therefore, linearly ac-
celerating to a climax that like a horizon is always there but
never happens.

But if the philosophers are prophets and the climactic
singularity is to be an event *within* history, rather than a
transformation of the structure of history from outside its
usual cultural frame of reference, then we should expect that

LOG OF EARTH

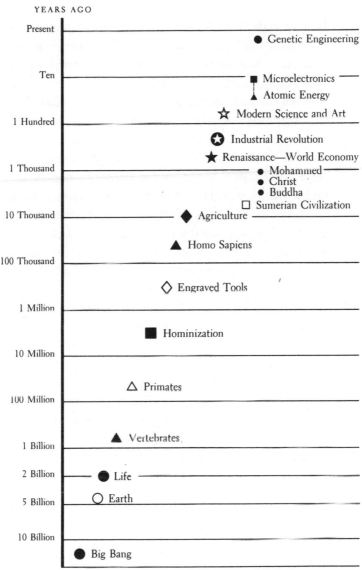

YEARS AGO

Present	● Genetic Engineering
Ten	■ Microelectronics
	▲ Atomic Energy
1 Hundred	☆ Modern Science and Art
	✪ Industrial Revolution
	★ Renaissance—World Economy
1 Thousand	● Mohammed
	● Christ
	● Buddha
	□ Sumerian Civilization
10 Thousand	◆ Agriculture
	▲ Homo Sapiens
100 Thousand	
	◇ Engraved Tools
1 Million	
	■ Hominization
10 Million	
	△ Primates
100 Million	
	▲ Vertebrates
1 Billion	
2 Billion	● Life
5 Billion	○ Earth
10 Billion	
	● Big Bang

SOURCE: Drs. E. Schwartz, W. I. Thompson, and F. Varela.

the acceleration of history will shortly bring about a situation in which major transformative events will begin to occur all at once, or within the time frame of months and weeks rather than decades and years.

What such a historical situation could be is hard to imagine, except for a person endowed with an apocalyptic imagination. One would have to envision a scenario in which the death of the forests, the Greenhouse Effect, the default of Latin American nations and collapse of the New York banks, the disintegration of the International Monetary Fund, the societal collapse of Mexico City, the explosion of several volcanoes, global famine, the use of nuclear weapons by terrorist groups in the Middle East and by dictators in South America, invasions, assassinations, that all of these were taking place while great works of art and new spiritual visions were animating the human race.

Many of the above events are already going on, but because they do not happen in the temporal mode of an event like Hiroshima, we do not see them as "happening." Consciousness works by exclusion as much as inclusion, and the price we seem to pay for organizing perception into the form of an "ego" is that the setting up of time seems to alienate most of the complex field of simultaneities that then have to erupt into the mental field of the ego in the form of revelations. The kind of people who do seem to be able to perceive the field of simultaneities are philosophers, mystics, artists, and paranoids. The metanoids seem content with an artistic form of expression that allows them to say many things at once, but the paranoids seem to take their own poetic insights literally. They pick up on simultaneities at the margins of consciousness, render them into imagery, and then try to read these tropes as if they were historical events. And so they sell their homes and wait to be picked up by flying saucers in the deserts of Arizona.

Artists, mystics, and philosophers, happy as they are in the life of words (perhaps because they are able to make a livelihood from words), do not seem to suffer from metaphors as much as paranoids do. These imaginative individuals can recognize that the transformations of history do not occur as events *in* history; they occur in myth. And so we should look to contemporary forms of mythology in art, philosophy, science fiction, and mysticism to see the recording of these meta-events that have been missed by the journalists of *Time* and *Die Zeit.*

The mythopoeic perception of history is not as difficult as it might seem at first, for artists since the Renaissance have been trying to teach us how to *see.* In 1480 Hieronymus Bosch painted *The Last Judgment;* in 1500, *The Temptation of Saint Anthony.* In one we see the sky cracking open and Jesus coming to judge the fallen world; in the other we see strange things flying in the air and dropping fire on burning cities. Well, for all of this prophetic anticipation of the aerial bombardment of Europe, the world did not end in 1500 and we still await the Second Coming. But from another point of view, the world-system did end in 1500. In the shift from medievalism to modernism, the centrifugal force of commerce spun outward toward a world economy and moved away from the center of the world ecclesia. No reporter living in 1500 could have "seen" this shift from one world-system to another, for it was not a historical event. It was a transformation, and the reporters of transformations are artists.

Marshall McLuhan has said that the artists are the early-warning systems for cultural change; so if we wish to understand the "Log of Earth" from another perspective, we should look around to find the Bosches of our own day.

One contemporary artist who is much taken with the historical relevance of mysticism and prophecy is the German composer Karlheinz Stockhausen. Shortly after the breakfast conversation with Francisco Varela and Eric Schwartz, I had occasion to attend the première of Stockhausen's *Jahreslauf* in Paris, and in this work I was startled to find a "synchronicity" to the "Log of Earth" and the comments of the Dalai Lama.

Jahreslauf is a theatrical as well as a musical piece, and what one sees is as important as what one hears. Above the performers is a large screen on which are seen flashing, like figures in an electronic calculator, the numbers of the changing years. At the front of the stage are four dancers performing movements from the Japanese martial art of karate. Each of the dancers moves at a different rate of speed: the dancer for the year, rapidly; for the decade, more slowly; for the century, even more slowly; and for the millennium, almost imperceptibly. From time to time the course of the years is brought to a halt, and tempters come on stage to try to distract the dancers from their appointed tasks. In this mythological version of the "punctuated equilibrium" of the evolutionists, the tempters themselves are absurd figures of basic human appetites: the cravings for food, for sex, and for power through technology. But each time the human comedy of the absurd threatens to stop the historical unfolding of time, an angel's face appears and sets all in motion again. Like stock figures in a medieval miracle play, the pull between the good and bad angels is expressed simplistically by the appearance on right and left stage of large, cardboard cartoon figures of a little girl and a bearded devil who peer in on the action from the sides of time. The figure of the devil appears at the moment of temptation and interruption, the figure of the childlike angel at the moment of rescue and the return of the cosmic dance.

At the rear of the stage, raised high above the dancers, are the musicians. In their formal black robes they seem like members of a religious order or judges of a tribunal sitting in judgment of human history. They are bathed in a magenta light, and we are told in the program notes that this light is very important for Stockhausen. He calls it the color of meditation:

> Each time I experience a high moment, whether it be playing or listening to music, I see violet-red. There is no form, just an extension of color like a blanket. And that sets me to breathing very slowly, that takes away breath and the beating of my heart.

The music played by the members of the tribunal has a haunting, unearthly quality to it; so the whole effect of the scene is to give the impression that one is looking at time on many levels at once, as if reading history were like reading a musical score.

Because the work is very much like a medieval miracle play, it has an allegorical quality that makes it seem rather

contrived. The dancers are the elemental angels who keep
the mystery of incarnation in movement; the clowns who
interrupt their movement are half-human, half-demon, and
entirely absurd. They inhabit a halfway region that is neither
angelic nor extraterrestrial, but human, all too human. Far
above them are the musicians, who play the unearthly, extraterrestrial music that is occultly linked to the events of
human history.

Human behavior, when framed in this context, a context
that is basically the esoteric religion of Stockhausen, takes
on a different meaning. Caught between the elemental level
below us, the angelic level above us, and the extraterrestrial
level far beyond our sense of perception, we cannot know
that the elementals dance to a music performed by the
hidden masters of the galaxy. At best, we humans follow our
petty appetites and delay the mysterious event toward which
all human time with its flashing numbers is flowing. And
then the present is reached, the numbers stop flashing on
the screen, the martial dancers give a shout, the musicians
a piercing note, and all finish in the end that seems a prelude
to the revelation of the "singularity."

Religious allegory seems an art form that is better suited
to times when people share a common faith, so I was not
confident that I had understood the work at one sitting.
Nevertheless, when I discussed *Jahreslauf* with Stockhausen
the day after its première, he seemed satisfied with my
interpretation, but he went even further in his explanation
of the unearthly music. Although I was not transported by
the beauty of the music, I was taken in, for the music was
familiar and yet strange, like a dream that one can remem-

ber but not recall. Stockhausen, however, identifies himself as one for whom "out of the body" experiences are not beyond recall. By his own admission, he comes from Sirius, a star renowned for its composers. Sirius is his true home, and it is not possible for him to accept the parochial world view of Earth. Life on this planet is for him an assignment, a form of Peace Corps work on what he calls a "karmic penal colony."

Idiosyncratic as Stockhausen may seem, his esoteric religion is not a unique and personal creation, for it has many elements in common with *The Book of Urantia* or the novels of Doris Lessing. As it so happened, I was that very day reading Lessing's *Shikasta,* a novel composed of the journals and reports of various extraterrestrials who take on the assignment of living on Earth to help our pathetic planet realign itself with the rest of the universe. When I asked Stockhausen about Doris Lessing, he said that he had never read any of her books. Whatever affinity they had in the *Zeitgeist,* they had no personal relationship at all.

Stockhausen is so much like the character Johor in Lessing's *Shikasta* that it seems a pity that Stockhausen and Lessing have never met. As different as the two of them are in personality and background, they do share a common mythopoeic sensibility. In her novels *The Four-Gated City, Briefing for a Descent into Hell, Memoirs of a Survivor,* and the *Shikasta* series, Lessing has presented a complete apocalyptic vision of the transition from one world-system to another. In her mediumistic way, she has anticipated the scientists' shift from geological uniformitarianism, the doctrine of Lyell and Darwin, to catastrophism. (This is a change that one can already see taking place more slowly in the pages of *The New Scientist* or in the Gaia Hypothesis of Lovelock and Margulis.[6]) In *Shikasta,* Earth is portrayed as an unstable planet given to instantaneous reversals of magnetic field, sudden ice ages, calamitous weather changes, and earthquakes and inundations on a plate-tectonic scale.

The concept of uniformitarianism in Victorian geology provided the stable crust on which the English could build the idea of progress that was so useful for the expansion of industrial society. But now that that expansion of industrial society has reached its limits, it is small wonder that, in the sociology of knowledge, the metaphysical foundations for industrialization are being eroded in a return to the doctrine of catastrophism. From colliding galaxies to supernovas to meteor bombardment, the picture of the universe in contemporary astrophysics is decidedly not a Victorian one in which Mother Nature behaves like an English queen.

Doris Lessing is not the only artist to express this change in world view. In his film *The Last Wave,* the Australian director Peter Weir explores the change in consciousness of a modern man who discovers the descriptive validity of apocalyptic prophecies. The hero of the film is a barrister in Sydney who discovers, in defending an aborigine, that his client's religion is not superstition, but cultural memory. The aborigines know the seasons of the cosmos, and while the European Australians are busy consuming, the aborigines know what time it is and what is about to happen. The point where the ancient and modern worlds meet is in the troubled consciousness of the barrister, who slowly begins to realize that the archaic mind is still alive in him, and that his personality is an incarnational mask worn by another being, a being whose mind fills with visions of the "last wave."

In his film *Picnic at Hanging Rock,* Weir also studies this difficult encounter between two world views, the archaic and the industrial. A few schoolgirls on a picnic stumble into some unexplained warp in space, a kind of Bermuda Triangle associated with a mysterious and ancient rock in the southeast corner of Australia, and then they simply disappear. This totally unexplainable event begins to derange the sensibilities of the good burghers of the girls' little rural town, and Weir dwells on the difficulties people have when they discover that human beings do not live in "reality," but merely in a socially conventional description of reality, and, in the case of the European Australians, a description that is incapable of dealing with the margins of experience.

Another young filmmaker who is fascinated with catastrophism and the Cassandra role of the prophet is the German director Werner Herzog. In his *Heart of Glass* he presents an image of a society in a state of shock and economic collapse. The secret of making ruby glass, the main industry of this eighteenth century town, has died with one of the elders, and so the whole economy built on this knowledge comes to a halt. In the town is a seer whose mind flashes, almost in an involuntary way, with visions of the future; his gift of second sight seems a derangement of the senses, a curse that alienates him from the rest of society. All the actors, except the seer, were hypnotized by Herzog, and so they move through the scenes reciting their lines in trance. The image of sleepwalkers moving about in trance while their community comes to a complete economic standstill is a haunting vision of the modern world in the eighties.

That Werner Herzog's imagination is drawn to images of catastrophism is clearly evident in his documentary *La Soufrière*. Hearing reports that an entire island in the Caribbean was about to explode in a volcanic eruption, Herzog rushed with his camera crew to the evacuated town to capture images of a world at the instant before annihilation. But nothing happened, and so the film became a study of an inevitable catastrophe that failed to take place. Herzog's ambivalence is clear at the end of the documentary, for he is relieved to be alive and disappointed that the catastrophe that attracted him in the first place was not available for an interview.

In *Heart of Glass* and *The Last Wave* both Herzog and Weir are fascinated with individuals of an archaic sensibility whose psychic gifts have remained intact in a capitalistic world that totally denies their validity. What Weir does with the prophecies of the aborigines, the American novelist Frank Waters does with the prophecies and myths of the Hopi of the American Southwest. In many ways, Peter Weir's *The Last Wave* is an Australian version of Frank Waters's and White Bear Fredericks's earlier work, *The Book of the Hopi*.

I have never had extensive talks with the elders of the Hopi nation, but their spokesman, Thomas Banyacya, came to Lindisfarne in Southampton in 1976 and there met with the High Lama from Tibet, Nechung Rinpoche. In the context of our conference, the Hopi and the Tibetan shared their ancient prophecies that a great war would rend the physical fabric of the earth, but that out of this destruction the relationship between the physical and etheric planes would be altered on earth, and the hitherto totally etheric city of Shambala and the realm of the *Kachinas* would materialize. These prophecies sounded like a Buddhist version of Bosch's painting of *The Last Judgment:* while warfare tears civilization apart, the sky cracks open and Jesus returns to establish the millennium.

So, as we can see, we don't really have to look very far to find the Hieronymus Bosches of our time. Whether we are dealing with a German composer, a Rhodesian novelist, a German or an Australian filmmaker, an American novelist and ethnographer, a Hopi leader, or a Tibetan Lama, we are dealing with the apocalyptic imagination of our era.

The world, of course, did not end in 1500, nor in 1984. In spite of a rash of apocalyptic prophecies in the period from 1979 to 1984, the world stumbled on, with all its cruelties and horrors still intact, with all its evil still unredeemed by the consummations of prophecy. Stockhausen's *Jahreslauf* announced some great cosmic revelation in 1979, but history did not quite seem up to what many psychics had expected of it. The Jupiter Effect came and went, and the English psychic Benjamin Cream's televised Second Coming had to be rescheduled. Atlantis did not rise in the Bahamas, California did not sink into the sea, the flying saucers did not bring back Melchizedek, Enoch, and Jesus; and Shambala stayed put.

A horizon provides an edge to our experience; if we move closer to it, it moves away, for it is not the *content* of our

experience but the *structure* of our knowing. And so it is
with myth and history. Myth is the horizon of history: in its
modality as the past, it is the world of legend; in its modality
as the future, it is the world of prophecy and science fiction.
If we try to move into this horizon bodily, to rent a flat in
Atlantis or freeze our bodies for later regeneration in some
future-perfect science in which death will have been conquered, we try to move into the horizon and eliminate the
sky to make it as prosaic, literal, and three-dimensional as
the ego. This form of psychic fundamentalism flattens out
experience to crush the multidimensionality of the universe.
Prophecies are to history what dreams are to one's waking
life; they are poetic renderings of the *implications* of our
experience. Precisely because consciousness is multidimensional, we need horizons, for there is always more "going on"
with us than what takes place in historical events or personal
conversations. The paranoid senses what he does not know
and then renders it into a poetry that he takes literally.
Nevertheless, there is often a poetic truth in the category-
mistakes of a paranoid vision that is missing in the reduc-
tionist schemata of scientific rationalism. The paranoid and
the artist sense that something very important has just happened to history, but they do not know how to cross over
the bitter gulf that separates art from politics, imagination
from economics.

It is easy now to look back on 1500 to see what Bosch was
driving at, but what are these Bosches of our era trying to
tell us? Are we dealing with the *de-structuring* of the modern
world-system intuited in mythological terms, or with the

impending *destruction* of our world, whether by thermonuclear war, pollution, or some plague brought on by a genetically engineered bacterium that did not behave as the scientists of agribusiness said it would?

I don't know. On Mondays, Wednesdays, and Fridays, I
think that we are experiencing a discontinuous transition
from one world-system to another, a "catastrophe." On
Tuesdays, Thursdays, and Saturdays, I feel better and think
that it is going to be a transition with continuity, one like
the previous transition from medievalism to modernism. On
Sundays, I try to rest and seek a contemplative detachment
from the vanities of scientific predictions or psychic revelations. If I am forced to choose one scenario over the other,
I would rather work politically for a cultural transformation
with continuity from one world-system to another, than join
a survivalist community or wait to be picked up by a flying
saucer.

But one of the valid functions of a horizon is to put the
foreground into perspective. If one sees history against a
horizon of myth, presumably, one sees more than if one's
nose is camping in the tent of the daily newspapers. Can the
narratives of the daily news and the narratives of the aeon
reveal similarities of theme and structure? Where can one
stand to see both the mythic backdrop to history and the
immediate foreground of the daily news?

Common sense would say that the best place to stand is
precisely at the point where both come into focus.

Nothing helps perception more than an edge. We cannot
see air unless it moves with wind and clouds. As Marshall

McLuhan was fond of saying, "I don't know who discovered water, but it certainly wasn't a fish." If we are inside an all-encompassing environment, we do not see it.

The all-encompassing environment for consciousness is noise.[7] The edge between noise and information, that turbulent shore, creates the atmosphere, the climate, the sky with life-giving rain. The rationalist mistakenly thinks that consciousness is limited to information, but the mystic and the artist know better. They know that consciousness is the erotic play of information with noise, with the recognizable, but immeasurable, shifting topologies of sea and sky.

If the all-encompassing environment for consciousness is noise, the all-encompassing environment for civilization is warfare. But just as consciousness cannot be limited to information, as the rationalist might wish, so *culture* cannot be limited to civilization, as the lawyer might wish. Writing and standing armies, clay tablets and mud walls, are entwined creations of the dawn of civilization. In hunting and gathering societies, and even in Neolithic agricultural villages, oral culture is aural culture: a world of the constant weaving back and forth between noise and information. But with the crystalization of information into writing, the edge between noise and information becomes hard and rigid: like a sword, like a clay tablet, like the walls of a fortress. No wonder that the beginning and end of the *Gilgamesh Epic* celebrate the walls of the city, the edges of civilization. But to force culture into civilization one must do violence to human nature, and so the new standing armies carry weapons to enforce written laws and to keep written maps of conquered territory.

The turbulent shore between human culture and the island of civilization is the space of violence; institutionalized violence in the form of warfare entirely surrounds civilization and defines it. Although we like to pretend that information does not like noise, it actually thrives on it; and although we like to pretend that governments do not like warfare, the entire organization of their various systems totally depends on it.

Pacifism is an emphasis on war precisely in the same manner in which celibacy is an emphasis on sexuality. In mind, as Gregory Bateson was fond of pointing out, the absence of a signal is a signal itself: if you don't send in your income tax, the feds will come to get you. Pacifism has not stopped war any more than celibacy has stopped fornication, precisely because in the contradictory nature of mind, negation is emphasis. If God says to Adam, "Look over here, Adam. Do you see this tree of knowledge with its red, luscious, juicy fruit? Well, don't eat it," God, being omniscient, is certainly aware that he has just put the thought of eating it into Adam's mind. This is what knowledge is all about, and affirmation and denial are merely the twinned modalities of emphasis.

This recognition changes the way we imagine the unconscious. Freud envisioned the unconscious as a coiled spring or a steam engine working through compression, but the unconscious can be seen merely as the reservoir of all negations in a culture. If you say, "Do not steal," you are creating an implicit shadow statement of "Steal." The collection of all these shadow statements is the unconscious: the space of forbidden knowledge.

Now, notice the isomorphism: rationalism says consciousness can be reduced to information; legalism says culture can be reduced to civilization; and priestcraft says that behavior can be reduced to moral codes. The pattern of emphasizing through negation, of course, sets up a structure in which humans are unconsciously formed to say one thing but do another; it becomes the only human way to deal with the contradictory nature of mind. And so humans praise peace, but organize their societies around warfare; praise marriage, but commit adultery; praise law, but hire lawyers to cheat on their income tax or get away with murder.

If we wish to work for a transformation of culture, we had better come to terms with these matters of mind. Pacifism will not eliminate war, and fundamentalisms will never eliminate the enemies they keep on creating. Intuition and common sense tell us that war is evil, but only knowledge can inform us that the transcendence of warfare requires the transcendence of civilization.

The conscious structure of the modern world is a collection of nation-states. The unconscious structure of the world is a dark ecology of warfare and terrorism; it is an enormously complex web of satellites and advanced informational systems living off the threat of war. Here again, God tried to warn us (Genesis 2:17): "For in the day that thou eatest thereof thou shalt surely die." It is not so much that death comes from knowledge, but that knowledge requires the perturbation at the edge, the disturbance at the shore, the difference. If we were gods in *samahdi*, with minds that were spheres whose interior surface was a mirror with no images tainted on its infinitely reflecting surface, we would have the mystic's or the *Daimon*'s "consciousness without an object," but we would not have knowledge. The price of the knowledge of good and evil is death; or, in another way of saying the same thing, time. The part of our consciousness that is multidimensional, or out of the ego's conventional construction of time and space, is the *Daimon.* [8] When the *Daimon* projects out of the time-less, space-less, undifferentiated world of the inward-mirroring sphere, it "falls" into a world of distinctions, a world of time, a world of limits. The limit to the life of a distinct thing is its death. The definition of a living thing is something that can die. The definition of a civilization is a system organized for warfare, for a social system of death.

But because human beings have minds, the reality for us is not matter, but information, and so the warfare state need not be constant destruction, but simply the idea of destruction. Actual wars could threaten the warfare system. Humans want just enough allusions to war to keep the society of warfare going. Actual thermonuclear war would threaten the whole global system of military integration and communication.

This irony is not as occult as it might seem, for take the case of the ballerina. Would we praise her art, her grace, her ability to leap, if gravity did not constantly pull at her with its limits? If humans had evolved as creatures in the weightless environment of space, you can be certain that classical ballet would not be the art form that they would develop. Ballet is the story of beauty and the beast: the lovely young thing and the horrible old beast that keeps pulling her down to earth. But beauty triumphs *because* of the beast, and what we celebrate is precisely her dance at the edge between freedom and restraint.

Warfare is the horrible old beast that keeps pulling civilization down, but until we recognize that humanity is the set of beauty *and* the beast, we will always set ourselves up for the oscillating rhythm of war and peace. Human beings will never disarm, for as long as they have minds in which difference and contradiction drive the system, just so long will they externalize a society in which the myth is the story of beauty and the beast. So, if we wish to have a new culture, we must have a transformation of consciousness: a discovery that the Buddha made when he returned to sit under the tree of Adam and Eve.

I make no claims to know what enlightenment is, but I have my hunches, and one of them is that enlightenment is a reversal of modes of awareness from ego to *Daimon.* From the point of view of the *Daimon* looking down, like Chaucer's Troilus on the battlefield of life, we are the whole field: slayer and slain, beauty and beast, information and noise. Children know this, for the beast interests them more than the beauty, and a story without good guys and bad guys would be a vapid tale indeed. Buddha asked why there was suffering; the philosopher asks why there is something instead of nothing. In other words, why does the *Daimon* fall, why does it choose to project an ego into an incarnation? Again, I make no claim to enlightened knowledge, but my hunch is that as the mirroring sphere of the *Daimon* passes through the plane of space-time, that plane, like a template, imprints distinct imagery and thoughts that now become reflected on the inside of the sphere as it passes out of incarnation, out of space and time. Perhaps, after a number of these passes through the plane of distinctions and death, or perhaps after only one passage, the encounter with the plane turns the sphere inside out, so that now it becomes a mirror reflecting its consciousness to the other spheres: not the windowless monads of Leibniz, but a multidimensional series of reflecting facets that could be called a grail.

Now you can see what I mean about the relationship between metanoia and paranoia, for my imagery *plays* with the edge of the permissible in making associations by metaphoric clusters. (Humor, and a self-deprecating sense of irony or whimsy, is "the difference that makes a difference" between metanoia and the more rigid and defensive paranoia.) But enough of hunches and speculations about enlightenment, for the transformation of consciousness needed to eliminate war need not be so distant a goal as the enlightenment of all sentient beings.

The New Age movement is not yet the politics of enlightenment, but it is a recognition that our global political condition does require a transformation of consciousness. The first stage in this transformation is to become more aware of the set of contradictions that constitutes civilization, for if we naively put forth a new list of commandments and call it New Age, we do nothing but redecorate the old structure. Such a seemingly revolutionary change, such as the change from the Shah to the Ayatollah in Iran, can often go from bad to worse. As New Age seekers become discontent with the noise and complexity of bourgeois democracies, they often eagerly surrender their painful minds to become the quiet subjects of a despotic Oriental guru whose satrapy is absolute and uniform. The guru and the devotee celebrate freedom from illusion, and enlightenment, but they practice deception and a dark form of psychic entrapment. The citizen and the politician celebrate civil order and international peace, but they practice ecological destruction and warfare. Conventionally, we call the ashram "New Age" and the nation-state "old age," but the mental structure operating in each context is the same.

The real secret of freedom seems to lie in the ability to deal with ambiguity, the capacity to tolerate noise and yet hear within its wild, randomizing abandon the possibilities of innovations and transformations. People with a low tolerance for noise seem to prefer the screamingly noisy but uniform and unambiguous world of Rajneeshpuram.

One of the first signs of spring in Bern is the amount of noise one hears on waking in the morning. With the return of the songbirds from Africa, the air fills with a thousand messages of change. But what are human beings signaling with their unconscious ecologies of noise? With ghetto-blasters and break-dancers on the streets, and MTV flowing twenty-four hours a day, humans in New York insist on communicating, even when it seems they have nothing to say.

Back and forth, like a yo-yo on a string, or like a jazz musician testing the furthest distance he can take from a melody and still relate to it, the electronic culture tests the edge between information and noise. Is this a signal that we are passing from the era of the collective unconscious (the age of industrialization and romanticism) to the era of the collective consciousness (an age of electronics and mysti-

cism)? If this sounds too far-out, let me give you the words
of a poetic scientist:

> We pass thoughts around, from mind to mind, compulsively
> and with such speed that the brains of mankind often ap-
> pear, functionally, to be undergoing fusion.
>
> This is, when you think about it, really amazing. The
> whole dear notion of one's own Self—marvelous, old free-
> willed, free-enterprising, autonomous, independent, isolated
> island of a Self—is a myth.
>
> We do not yet have a science strong enough to displace
> the myth. If you could label, by some equivalent of radioac-
> tive isotopes, all the bits of human thought that are con-
> stantly adrift, like plankton, all around us, it might be possi-
> ble to discern some sort of systematic order in the process,
> but, as it is, it seems almost certainly random. There has to
> be something wrong with this view. It is hard to see how we
> could be in possession of an organ so complex and intricate
> and, as it occasionally reveals itself, so powerful, and be using
> it on such a scale just for the production of *a kind of back-
> ground noise.* [Emphasis added.] Somewhere, obscured by
> the snatches of conversations, pages of old letters, bits of
> books and magazines, memories of old movies, and the
> disorder of radio and television, there ought to be more
> intelligible signals.
>
> Or perhaps we are only at the beginning of learning how
> to use the system, with almost all of our evolution as a
> species still ahead of us . . .
>
> The mechanism is there, and there is no doubt that it is
> already capable of functioning, even though the total yield
> thus far seems to consist largely of bits . . . There may be
> some laws about this kind of communication, mandating a
> critical density and mass before it can function with effi-
> ciency. Only in this century have we been brought close
> enough to each other, in great numbers, to begin the fusion

around the earth, and from now on the process may move rapidly.[9]

The rise of the modern world-system most certainly did come about with the appearance of new forms of communication through print and a stable, trans-European postal service that enabled scholars and artists to use the pathways for messages set up by bankers. With hindsight we now call this network of bankers like Cosimo de Medici and scholars like Marsilio Ficino, the Renaissance.

And what was true for the Renaissance was even truer for the Enlightenment. The increase in the speed of transatlantic shipping enabled Franklin and Jefferson to turn the New World into a proving ground for the new liberal thought. The scholarly and scientific academies of Europe encouraged the growth of the American Philosophical Society in Philadelphia, and it was this important society that helped to translate new and revolutionary ideas into new and revolutionary polities.

Now, with telephones, modems, and personal computers linked to satellite networks such as The Source, individuals and not just institutions are able to communicate with their colleagues around the world. New coffee houses, salons, or what anthropologist Margaret Mead liked to call "sapiential circles" have emerged and are flashing ideas back and forth across the spaces that used to divide them. Just as print and the political pamphlet empowered the hitherto powerless working class, so now electronic forms of communication have given new powers to the hitherto powerless "alternative movement."

What has emerged in this alternative movement is not so much an ideology, which, like nineteenth-century Marxism, is more of an expression of the literary elites and working classes of industrial society, but an ecology of consciousness. Like different wild grasses in a prairie rather than the monocrop of corn in an agribusiness farm, the differences in culture do not seem to break up the unity. From the conservers of Oregon to the more preachy and pious readers of *Resurgence* in Great Britain to the more strident and anarchistic Greens of West Germany, the alternative movement manages to be coherent without the collectivizing force of an ideology.

Ironically enough, though the United States has influenced the relaxed blue-jeans lifestyle of this culture, it has shown very little political evolution. Jerry Brown was profoundly influenced by E. F. Schumacher and Gregory Bateson, and he tried to take a few of their ideas into his campaign for the American presidency in 1980, but he failed; and the country, following Great Britain's shift to Thatcher, swung back to the far right with Ronald Reagan. In the presidential campaign of 1984 there were no new ideas whatsoever, and although Gary Hart talked about the need for a "reconceptualization of the Democratic Party," both he and the party have been unable to think out just what that might mean.

The failures of Jerry Brown and Gary Hart seem to come from an inherent limitation built into media politics, for both men suffered from the dilemma of playing the chameleon on a Scotch plaid: they did not know what color to adopt to ensure their survival.

Music seems to be more effective in getting a message through an electronic culture than political campaigns. Political leaders are really followers of polls and trends, and so a presidential campaign does not seem to be an effective instrument for cultural transformation. Ideas and slogans, programs and crusades, these seem to be the hangovers from the days of oratory, rhetoric, and speeches: the days of Abraham Lincoln or William Jennings Bryan. The considerable skill of Ronald Reagan seems to come from his actor's sensitivity to an audience. Jimmy Carter and Teddy Kennedy were seriously intent—the one pious, the other fervent—but both failed to appreciate that in a media culture, ideas don't count, or vote. Reagan is always wrong but never mistaken in his understanding that the American presidency is a role and not a task. Jimmy Carter was a serious *Homo faber*, but Reagan is *Homo ludens* with a juggler's instinctive feeling for the play of images in an electronic society. Here again, we have to pay due respect to Marshall McLuhan, who was the first to see that the content of a communication is not what the communication is truly about. The content of Ronald Reagan is small-town, midwestern, Protestant, and fiscally conservative America, but he, much more than the threatening Zen Governor Brown, has been the one to effect the shift from New York to Los Angeles, from Europe to the Pacific Basin, from steel mills to space shuttles and Star Wars. Just as Nehru put Gandhi's picture on every wall in India and then led the nation away from cottage industries to capital-intensive economies of scale and nuclear reactors, so Reagan invoked every platitude of the *Reader's Digest* in the very act of calming

Middle America as he put them to the side of history.

If the American presidency with its permanent presidential media campaign is a human role and not an inhuman task, then the culture cannot be shaped or transformed by the office. The presidency can only reflect back, in comfort and nostalgia, to the mass mind what its society used to be. A more profound political strategy would be to work to transform the cultural context in which politicians are constrained to work.

Charles Péguy has said, *"Tout commence en mystique et finit en politique."* From this point of view, it is very clear that the United States, unlike West Germany, is still very much in the phase of the *mystique.* Planetary culture and politics are still very much a matter of myth, religion, and art, expressed more in films like *Koyaanisqatsi* or operas like *Satyagraha* than in presidential campaigns.

In the 1970s places like Lindisfarne in New York, the Zen Center in San Francisco, and the Center for Intercultural Documentation (CIDOC) in Cuernavaca served as intellectual coffee houses that brought together people who were neither Old Left nor New Right, the thinkers and practitioners of a new "alternative" political configuration. Now, ten years after John and Nancy Todd first met Gregory Bateson at Lindisfarne,[10] that intellectual configuration still makes a good deal of sense, for it is a *natural* movement to start with the epistemology of Bateson and show how it relates to the Taoist ecology of the Todds, and then go on to show how epistemology and ecology can come together in the economics of E. F. Schumacher, Hazel Henderson, and Paul Hawken. And since economic behavior is directly related to energy consumption and architecture, it is no great jump to move from the thinking of these solar-age economists to the work of Amory and Hunter Lovins and Sim Van der Ryn. Since energy grids have often been the structures with which a powerful center has colonized a peripheral culture, we then discover that perceptions of energy flow enable us to see bioregionalism in a new way: either through the re-*visioning* of agriculture with Wes Jackson and Gary Nabhan, or through the poetry of Wendell Berry and Gary Snyder. When all of these people met and continued to meet at Lindisfarne in New York or Colorado, they embodied New Age politics in two critical ways: they had no leader and they had no ideology; what they had was an ethos and a recognition that they were all part of a larger ecology of consciousness.[11]

For me, this shift from followership to fellowship, from an ideology controlled by an elite to an ecology of consciousness embodied through differentiation, is the *sine qua non* of New Age politics. If the Greens turn ecology into ideology, they will lose the new way of thinking and simply become fundamentalists of an antitechnological persuasion. Now the Greens are, as they say, not Left or Right, but "ahead," but if they become a nativistic movement, they will simply become another Ghost Dance. The world is too complex and culturally diverse to be ruled by any fundamentalist ideology, Christian or Islamic, Marxist or Green. Everywhere around the world now one can see the failure of ideologies and the cruelties of fundamentalisms. Ideologies, with their lack of flexibility, with their inability to play with noise and information, simply cannot deal with the innovative spontaneities of life.

The Zen or alchemical ability to entertain opposites in consciousness is the mode of non-ideological thinking. Mysticism and technology, socialism and capitalism, all have their places in a planctary culture. However, we have been trained to think of "us and them," to turn prairies into monocrops, and to turn cities into freeways and parking lots; so we need to be untrained to see the shape opposites actually take in a polity. What I wish to propose next would be better understood if experienced as a computer-animated video, but such a costly form of communication is only made available to rock stars. Intellectuals are constrained to black-and-white books, so readers have to strain to take in print what appear to be abstract models and deterministic descriptions; but if they were rendered with computer animation and video synthesizers, one could see clearly that these ideas are the imaginative play and the performance of archetypal patterns in ordinary contexts. Perhaps some day the colorful models of the next chapter will find their appropriate technology, but for the moment, I pass them on to show the shape of opposites in politics—or to be Greek and philosophical, the nature of an *enantiomorphic* polity—and to unfold what I mean by an ecology of consciousness. Ultimately, politics unbound from ideology is another phrase for the spring of life.

Notes

1. In an earlier version of this book, published as a pamphlet by the Findhorn Foundation in 1982, I did rather naively imagine that some sort of Planetary Constitutional Convention was a possibility for the future. That pamphlet version was based upon lectures I gave at Findhorn in December of 1979, and so I focused on such current events as Jerry Brown's campaign for the American presidency and Zbigniew Brzezinski's leadership of the Trilateral Commission. In entirely rewriting FROM NATION TO EMANATION and doubling the length of the manuscript, I have changed my mind as I have watched the rise of Christian and Islamic fundamentalisms. I can see now that a Planetary Constitutional Convention is too ethnocentric a projection, too derivative from Western Enlightenment values. I have tried to darken my excessively bright New Age projections to bring the perspective more in line with the world of Khomeini's Iran, Thatcher's Great Britain, and Reagan's United States of America. I have also taken out some esoteric material that, in pamphlet form, was intended only for the specific context of the Findhorn Foundation's interest in the Western esoteric tradition.

2. Ouranos is castrated with a sickle, a crescent-shaped tool that is symbolic of the moon and the lunar cosmology of women's mysteries; so the Greek myth can be seen to express a memory trace of the old conflict of man the hunter and woman the gatherer. Interestingly enough, the young men side with their mother, Gaia, to castrate the old god. For the reference to

the original, see HESIOD'S THEOGONY, trans. Richmond Lattimore (Ann Arbor: University of Michigan Press, 1959), lines 153–168, p. 132.

3. See René Thom, STRUCTURAL STABILITY AND MORPHOGENESIS, trans. D. H. Fowler (Reading, Mass.: W. A. Benjamin, 1975).

4. See Henry Adams, THE EDUCATION OF HENRY ADAMS (New York: Simon & Schuster, 1957).

5. See Michel Foucault, THE ORDER OF THINGS (New York: Vintage, 1973), p. 386.

6. See James E. Lovelock and Lynn Margulis, "The Gaia Hypothesis," CO-EVOLUTION QUARTERLY, Summer 1975, pp. 30–40; see also James E. Lovelock, GAIA: A NEW LOOK AT LIFE ON EARTH (Oxford: Oxford University Press, 1979).

7. Because of his participation in the original Macy Conferences that helped to articulate the new science of cybernetics, Gregory Bateson maintained a lifelong fascination with the role of noise in innovation. Consider his comment "All that is not information, not redundancy, not form and restraints —is noise, the only possible source of *new* patterns." See "Cybernetic Explanation" in Gregory Bateson, STEPS TO AN ECOLOGY OF MIND (New York: Ballantine, 1972), p. 410.

Recently, the Parisian philosopher Michel Serres has begun to elaborate his own approach to the role of noise in culture. Consider his comment *"Le bruit est le fond de l'information, la matière de cette forme"* ("Noise is the basis of information, the matter of this form") from his Genese (Paris: Grasset, 1982), p. 22. Or see his remark *"S'il existe un fond des choses et du monde, c'est le bruit de fond"* ("If there is a base of things and the world, it is background noise.") in his Hermes V: Le Passage du Nord-Quest (Paris: Les Editions de Minuit, 1980), p. 157.

8. *Daimon* is the word Socrates used to describe his inner guide; it is a word that Yeats picked up and elaborated into an entire theory of incarnation in his book A VISION. The ego melts away under the heat of introspection, but the temperature at which the *Daimon* melts into Emptiness is, to speak metaphorically, much higher.

9. See Lewis Thomas, LIVES OF A CELL (New York: Viking, 1974), pp. 142–144.

10. See John Todd's and Gregory Bateson's talks reprinted in EARTH'S ANSWER: EXPLORATIONS OF PLANETARY CULTURE AT THE LINDISFARNE CONFERENCES (New York: Harper & Row/Lindisfarne, 1977). For an example of Bateson's influence on the Todds' theory of design, see Nancy Jack Todd and John Todd, BIOSHELTERS, OCEAN ARKS, CITY FARMING: ECOLOGY AS THE BASIS OF DESIGN (San Francisco: Sierra Club Books, 1984).

11. Some of the meetings of the Lindisfarne Fellows were transcribed and published in the LINDISFARNE LETTER from 1975 to 1982; other lectures or conferences are available only on cassette recordings. Many of these early explorations have since been made available in book form, as, for example, in Gregory Bateson's MIND AND NATURE (New York: E. P. Dutton, 1979) and Francisco Varela's PRINCIPLES OF BIOLOGICAL AUTONOMY (New York: Elsevier-Holland, 1979). The other material is available from The Lindisfarne Press, R.D. 2, West Stockbridge, MA 01266.

CHAPTER

From Nation
to Emanation

*A*n ecology is a form of life in which opposites coexist. *Eco* means "home," and *logos* means "word"; ecology is thus the home word that enables us to return to earth in a homeward direction and know it truly for the first time. "In the beginning was the Word," and more is meant there by "Word" than simply an Old Man in a nightie screaming *"Fiat lux!"* A word is a cabbalistic vibratory signature that holds the code of identity for a universe, a galaxy, a star, a planet, a person, a molecule. Adam, before the Fall, was the perfect *scientist* (literally, "one who knows") who gave creatures their proper names, because he had the ability to recognize the implicit word that was at the beginning of each being. Recently, postlapsarian man in a space suit has been able to look homeward to see the earth truly. Both American astronauts and Russian cosmonauts have described the experience of mystical connection they felt by looking homeward from outer space. They could not see boundaries or ideologies, but they could see oceans and continents and know that it is not the case that the continent is right and the ocean wrong. The true relationship between these opposites is through a reconciliation at the higher level of the atmosphere in which the clouds bring the moisture of the ocean to the continent in the form of rain. As it is now with the ecosystem, so shall it have to become with the political system.

Truth cannot be expressed in an ideology, for Truth is that which overlights the conflict of opposed ideologies. A global polity cannot be simply capitalist or communist, Christian or Muslim, natural or technological, and the effort of one ideology to extend itself infinitely, only extends indefinitely the violent conflict of all against each. As the poet W. B. Yeats expressed it on his deathbed, "Man can embody the truth but he cannot know it."[1] The Truth cannot be known in an ideology, but it can be embodied in an ecology; anything less does violence to human nature and human culture.

Violence is, of course, exactly what we are now doing to nature and culture, and the logical extension of our modern world view is the poisoning of earth, air, and water, and the transformation of every smoggy, slum-filled city into a war-torn Beirut. We know this, but we do not stop it; for mere *knowing* does not start or stop anything, and that is why Yeats said that man cannot *know* the Truth. The embodiment of the Truth is the ecology, the home word, the body politic.

I may be New Age, but I am not so naive as to think that a new planetary culture will come into being intellectually or peacefully. The soul of our age is Dionysian, not Apollonian, and we need to remember that the child Dionysus did not have a natural birth. Semele, his mother, lusted after godhood, so that in revenge, Hera put it into Semele's mind to ask her lover Zeus to reveal himself completely to her. Though Zeus tried to reason with Semele, in order to spare her the vision that would destroy her integrity as a human being, she would not listen but held her immortal lover to his promise. The vision of Zeus in his transcendent nature destroyed Semele, and into her shattered womb Zeus reached to bring out his son, the god Dionysus.

And so it is now with us, for the religions lust after God; but like wives in a harem, they fight among themselves as to who is the favorite. And the scientists don't deliver us from religious madness, for they do not wish to mate with God; they wish to *be* God, to have the power to tinker with nature and take command of evolution through genetic engineering. So there is no escaping it: religious warfare will continue, and the war against nature will continue. But religious warfare will continue to sicken humanity in disgust at the hysterical fanaticisms of zealots of all convictions, and the increasing poisoning of the earth will continue to sicken a generation for whom industrial civilization will not work simply because for them there will be no work.

As the ecological crisis begins to inform our perceptions to enable us to see just how ecologies live, we will begin to understand from far too many Belfasts and Beiruts that any polity has to be an interaction of opposites. In a polity that has the shape of opposites, an *enantiomorphic* polity, the prophetic wisdom of William Blake's "In opposition is true friendship" will be finally understood politically and not just poetically.

Values are not objects; they are relationships. When you overlay one pattern with another, a third pattern emerges, a *moiré* pattern. In egoistic thought an individual thinks that the opinion he holds is right and that all others are wrong. The zealot dehumanizes his enemies and sees them as devils. The Ayatollah Khomeini is a classic example of the zealot, for he always characterizes his opponents as devils and agents of Satan. But the person who goes around screaming about possession by the devil is usually the one who has been taken over by a hatred that has killed his own capacity for love, compassion, and understanding. A man who sends the Kurds to the firing squad is one who, in spite of being a mullah, has never taken to heart the opening of the Koran: "In the name of Allah, the compassionate, the merciful . . ."

All through their history, Jews, Christians, and Moslems have killed in the name of Jahweh, Christ, and Allah, but this transformation of consciousness into an ideology is not the higher, esoteric wisdom of the Abrahamic religions. An ideology, religious or political, is a form of possession, and as such it is a possession of the ego. The state of consciousness of the *Daimon* (or in Persian Zoroastrianism, *daena*) is one of compassion, love for one's enemy, and a global awareness that above the battle field is a single sun. The sun does not say that the rose is right and the dandelion is wrong. A politics based on anything less than this knowledge is fatal.

Had the Ayatollah Khomeini understood the principles

of an enantiomorphic polity, he would have, like Gandhi, remained a figure of religious authority and turned over power to Barzaghan. But he did not exercise the nonego religious detachment of a Sufi; he became passionate, ignorant, and violently attached to his revolution, his opinions, his Iran. By operating at this lower, willful level of the ego, the Ayatollah remained at the level of the remorseless, mindless, and unconscious working of fate, of karma. Those who cannot create their destiny in consciousness will have their fate inflicted upon them in unconsciousness. At this level the karmic mechanism of the *enantiodromia* plays out its law of opposites: you become what you hate. In the early days of the Iranian Revolution, the Ayatollah in Paris was a figure of authority and the Shah in Tehran was a figure of power. With the success of the revolution, the positions were reversed and the Ayatollah became a new kind of tyrannical shah. Humanity never seems to learn this lesson, for whether we are looking at Cromwell, Robespierre, Lenin, or Khomeini, the tragic irony remains the same: revolution is a change of faces, but not a change of consciousness.

If one does have an appreciation of the phenomenology of opposites in which we become what we hate, then a politics of compassion, as contrasted with a politics of violent conflict, begins to become a cultural possibility. In the shift from mindless, passionate conflict to mindful, dispassionate balancing, we move from agony to *agon*. One Lindisfarne Fellow, E. F. Schumacher, came very close to expressing the principles of the enantiomorphic polity in his last work before his death:

The pairs of opposites, of which *freedom and order* and *growth and decay* are the most basic, put tension into the world, a tension that sharpens man's sensitivity and increases his self-awareness. No real understanding is possible without awareness of these pairs of opposites which permeate everything man does.

In the life of societies there is the need for both justice and mercy. "Justice without mercy" said Thomas Aquinas, "is cruelty; mercy without justice is the mother of dissolution," a very clear identification of a divergent problem. Justice is a denial of mercy, and mercy is a denial of justice. Only a higher force can reconcile these opposites: wisdom. The problem cannot be solved, but wisdom can transcend it. Similarly, societies need stability *and* change, tradition *and* innovation, public interest *and* private interest, planning *and* laissez-faire, order *and* freedom, growth *and* decay. Everywhere society's health depends on the simultaneous pursuit of mutually opposed activities or aims. The adoption of a final solution means a kind of death sentence for man's humanity and spells either cruelty or dissolution, generally both.[2]

Schumacher's insight about the nature of opposites in social dynamics is not idiosyncratic, but part of a phenomenology of life that is also beginning to be understood in biology. In Professor Henri Atlan's recent synthesis of information theory and biology, the phenomenology of opposites that both Schumacher and I are arguing for is seen as part of the dynamics of all living systems:

So then, it would suffice to look at organization as an uninterrupted process of disorganization-reorganization, and not as a state, so that order and disorder, the organized and the contingent, construction and destruction, life and death, are

no longer so distinct. And moreover that is not all of it.
These processes where the unity of opposites—such a unity
is not realized as a new state, a synthesis of the thesis and
the antithesis, it is the movement of the process itself which
constitutes the "synthesis"—these processes cannot exist
except that the errors are *a priori* true errors, that order at
any given moment is truly disturbed by disorder, that destruction (though not totally realized) is still real, that the
irruption of the event is a veritable irruption (a catastrophe
or a miracle or both). In other words, these processes which
appear to us as one of the foundations of living beings, the
result of a sort of collaboration between what one cus-
tomarily calls life and death, can only exist precisely when
it is not a question of cooperation but always radical opposition and negation.[3]

Henri Atlan, the French Algerian Jew living in Jerusalem,
has a very tragic view of the necessity of opposition; but it
would seem to me that it is when liberal cooperation is naive
that it annihilates true distinctions and thus causes violence
to express the distinction. When an ecosystem is destroyed
by humans, that is when nature becomes destructive in flood
and forest fire, and invasions of pests come to reveal the
distinctions we have annihilated in our monocrop mentality.
Precisely because the Palestinians were eliminated, they
now seek to annihilate Israel. The cultural ecology of the
Middle East cannot be an Israeli monocrop without the
perpetual need for military force to subdue all differences.

And so Atlan's "radical opposition and negation" if it is
to be truly rooted, as the word *radical* or *radix* would de-
mand, has to become the preservation of information in the
affirmation of differences.

Whenever the violently exhausted world is ready for a world *parlement* that is not a world-state's parliament, then the founding mothers and fathers of a real New Age will have to have just such an understanding of the phenomenology of opposites in which "opposition is true friendship."

To suggest another way of looking at the field of interacting opposites, I would like to use the traditional image of the Quaternity to present a geometrical version of William Blake's "Fourfold Vision."

Let us begin with the most basic opposition of *Cosmos* and *Chaos*. *Cosmos* comes from the Greek word *kosmeo*, meaning "to set up" or "to arrange"; thus *Cosmos* is an arrangement, an order set up against the force of *Chaos*, the force pulling order toward entropy. (See Appendix, Figure 1, The Two Modes of Existence.)

Cosmos and *Chaos*, or order and entropy, is the fundamental duality of existence. To express this ontology mythologically, we can say that God the Father is beyond all manifestation, beyond what the human mind knows as existence, the world of distinctions and differences; and so for "mind" Godhead is indescribable and unknowable. Only consciousness without a sensory construction, consciousness without an object, can become aware of this level of Being that is the *Gotheit* of Meister Eckhart or the Emptiness of Buddhism. But as the *Daimon* projects an ego into time and space, so in a parallel form of manifestation does Divinity project into creation. This creative God generates forms, and with them shadows, for with the production of distinct things comes limits, comes death, comes the space of freedom that allows evil to come into being. Milton recognized this necessity, for in *Paradise Lost,* as Lucifer is meditating that "one step higher makes me highest," God the Father announces the emanation of the Son. Christ and Lucifer, Demiurge and Gnostic Archon, are the twin modalities of manifestation. Since to ex-ist is to stand out from Being as *a* being, to exist as a distinct form immediately calls forth its opposite, its negation. The Devil, therefore, is the force that abhors existence and seeks to destroy it. Or, in the words of Goethe's Mephistopheles: "The spirit I, that endlessly denies,/And rightly too; for all that comes to birth/Is fit for overthrow, as nothing worth."[4]

But as negation must always be bound to the object it denies, just as a shadow is bound to its form by the light, so evil can never be a creative force; it can only be destructive, imitative, or negative. And so, in the conventional wisdom, we say that "The Devil is the ape of God"; or, *"Demon, Deus inversus est."* The nothingness of Satan is therefore an ignorant parody of the Emptiness of God the Father. The consummation of the opposition of Christ and the Devil within the universe is expressed in the third person of the Trinity, the Holy Spirit.

If these mythological and theological terms seem arcane, that is because, like the Romans who renamed the old Greek gods, we moderns have renamed the old medieval gods and prefer to speak about entropy and the Second Law of Thermodynamics; and, also like the Romans, we do not often accept that our religion is still a form of mythology. Science has renamed the old gods, but under the names of force, entropy, information, and noise, the old gods still speak

through these masks of new personalities, for that is what
persona means: *per sona,* to sound through. Myth and science, therefore, are not oppositions like falsehood and truth,
but rather, like epic and tragedy, simply two different performances of the narratives of human identity.

To return to myth, in the dialectic between *Cosmos* and
Chaos, two mediations of the modes of existence arise:
Charisma and *Routine* (terms I am taking from Max
Weber's sociology of religion). (See Figure 2, The Two
Mediations of the Modes.) In *Charisma,* literally meaning
"divine gift," innovation is introduced into a system, and
this is both ordering and destabilizing. In *Routine,* an innovation is maintained and newer innovations are resisted; so
Routine is stabilizing, but because of its rigidity in a world
of time, its stabilizing quality is ultimately destabilizingly
brittle. And so we can see that in the world of manifestation,
the world of *Charisma* and *Routine,* one's unique excellence
(areté) is also one's tragic flaw *(hamartia).* *Charisma* is the
energizing spirit; *Routine* is the receptive condition that
accepts things as they are. In mythology, this pair would be
expressed in the opposition of Seth and Osiris. Osiris is the
innovative cultural hero who creates agriculture and the arts
of civilization, but Seth is the old Paleolithic reactionary
with his beloved flint tools who seeks to frustrate Osiris's
mission and trap him in the coffin of brute, resistant matter.[5] This opposition should not be seen simply as a battle
of good and evil, and therefore I have not made the colors
in the model black and white, but gold and blue. *Charisma*
is grace, the bestowal of divine gifts, the liberation from the
unconscious and mechanical movement of matter and time

and the laws of karma. Routine is the nature of form, the laws of karma.

When you superimpose the two triangles of *Charisma* and *Routine* onto the two triangles of *Cosmos* and *Chaos*, you can see the Basic Quaternity, the "Fourfold Vision," as shown in Figure 3. These four triangles then generate, in their overlapping patterns, numerous other triangles. The Quaternity can thus be seen to be an archetype, an atemporal crystal from the level of Plato's world of forms that, when "dropped" into the plane of manifestation, generates what we perceive as history.

To focus on one set of triangles within the Quaternity, consider Figure 4, The Four Faculties with Their Associated Tones of Consciousness.

In the esoteric mythology of Theosophy, each of these levels of awareness has its center of focus on a plane of being, and this center of being can be reified to be conventionally described as a "subtle body." The *Daimon* is focused on the Causal Plane, but the lower levels of the Causal Plane overlap with the top of the Mental Plane, and this is the realm of the archetypes. The Basic Quaternity or crystal that I am here describing is an archetypal form from this level of awareness, or plane of being. The bottom of the Mental Plane overlaps with the top of the Astral Plane. The archetypal world of forms is the realm of the illumined mind; it is the meeting place of the Causal and Mental Planes, a place of music and geometry that is alluded to in our world in works such as Bach's *Art of the Fugue* or the Cathedral of Chartres. Similarly, the meeting place of the Mental Plane and the Astral Plane, the plane of the emotions, is heaven or paradise; it is a place of tranquility and rest. The bottom of the Astral overlaps with the top of the Physical Plane, and this is the place of harmony and grace, the etheric plane, the plane of the dancer, the balanced *chi* of the master of Tai Chi Chuan, the unity of heart and body in superb athletes or in the sexual ecstasy of sublimely paired lovers.

These four overlapping planes of Causal, Mental, Astral, and Physical are like quantum steps of energy; therefore the conventional language that talks about the Causal Body or the Astral Body does tend to encourage what the philosopher A. N. Whitehead called "misplaced concreteness." Perhaps a candle flame is a better image of interpenetrating energies than bodies and can serve as a metaphor for the individual being. The blue part of the flame close to the wick is the Physical Plane; above it is the gold of the darker, intermediate region, the Astral Plane, and above that is the gold of the Mental Plane. At the pointed crest of the flame is the meeting place of the individual flame and the more universal gaseous envelopment of the atmosphere that makes the flame possible in the first place. The crest is a good metaphor for the *Daimon,* the point where the unique and the universal come together, for the Causal Plane is at once the beginning of individual manifestation and the closest point to universal Being, for beyond the Causal Plane is the Atman-Brahman of the Hindus, or the even less reified relational Emptiness of the Buddhists.

If these religious terms cause individuals of a more conventional scientific orientation serious difficulties, then one can simply regard these terms as mythological narratives for neurological states of attention. Attention to the physical body is conventional perception; attention to the psyche, either in trance or dreams, is the shamanistic mode of perception; attention to pure logical processes and structures without sensory content is the mental mode of perception, a state familiar to mathematicians (for when Whitehead was deep in concentration on mathematical problems he became entirely oblivious of his surroundings, which is a state of trance similar to yogic concentration or *pratyahara*); consciousness without an object, without either a sensory perception or a mathematical or logical construction, is the mode of the *Daimon*, a holographic mode in which unique and universal are not horizonally defined.

For the materialist, all of these states are functions of the brain, and the consciousness of the *Daimon* would be seen as deep, dreamless sleep. For this sort of materialist, the brain produces thoughts and the kidneys produce urine. For the shaman, the mathematician, or the mystic, it feels more as if the brain were a projection of Mind, something like the way that a snail extrudes a shell. For the mystic, Mind is not an object located in three-dimensional space; therefore, knowledge is available in modes of hyperdimensionality. The psychic materialist tends to reify this mode of attention and talks about an "astral body bound to the physical body by a silver cord," but this is to use the arrangement of one dimensional system as a metaphor for another; it is the same category-mistake as regarding thoughts as the urine of the brain.

Societies at different times have favored one mode of attention over another to give it cultural authority, for there are four value orientations that derive from the four faculties. Theocratic societies, such as Vedic India or Pharaonic Egypt, have tried to express these four value orientations in a rigid hierarchy of four castes: the ruling class, the mental or priestly class, the warrior and artisan class, and the slave class. Once again, this caste system can be seen to be a faulty reification that comes from the human weakness for "misplaced concreteness." On the turn of the historical spiral into a New Age, we do not need to be that simplistic any longer. The four value orientations can be seen to be social processes that become institutionalized in political parties. (See Figure 5, The Four Value Orientations.)

In Figure 5 the dynamics of each political party are suggested through the relationship of position and color. The purple of *Cosmos* and the blue of *Routine* are mediated in the line that connects them and creates the color of deep indigo. The triangle of the Conservative is at its widest point in the beginning of its structural alignment between *Cosmos* and *Routine,* but as it goes forth to engage its opposition in the field of political dynamics, it moves toward its opposite, and thus the triangle approaches the vanishing point in the quadrant of the Radical. This dialectical movement in which a force, in its fullest development, turns into its opposite is called the *enantiodromia,* a concept from ancient alchemy that was reintroduced into modern thought by C. G. Jung. Opposite to the Conservative is the Radical; here an alignment between the gold of *Charisma* and the red of *Chaos* is created, and this generates the orange triangle of the Radical, which is at its widest in its own quadrant, but as it goes forth into the field of political opposition, its power winds down to approach the point of nothingness in the quadrant of its opposite, the Conservative. Constrained at Left and Right by Liberal and Reactionary, the Radical is unable to make the field of political action a pure and complete expression of its own ideology. In the Liberal quadrant an alignment is created between the gold of *Charisma* and the purple of *Cosmos* in the green triangle.

Hemmed in by Conservative and Radical, the internal poles of the Liberal position, the Liberal individual goes forth into the field of political action and eventually winds down into the point of the opposite position, the Reactionary. Interestingly enough, this was seen in the 1980 American presidential election, for such former Liberals as Norman Podhoretz and Irving Kristol became the leading apologists for Ronald Reagan. (Notice that they did not become Conservatives of the Gerald Ford persuasion, but Reactionaries of the Reagan ideology.) In the quadrant of the Reactionary an alignment between the blue of *Routine* and the red of *Chaos* is created that generates the magenta triangle of the Reactionary. The Reactionary resists innovation and so is attracted to the values of *Routine;* but like the Radical he cannot stand the status quo and wishes to disrupt the system, and so he is equally attracted, in rhetoric at least, to the values of *Chaos.* In 1980 Ronald Reagan talked about disbanding the Departments of Energy and Health, Education, and Welfare, but as the purity of his own rhetorical ideology encountered the field of political action, the magenta triangle of the Reactionary wound down toward the point of its opposite in the Liberal quadrant. Thus Reagan as president, very much like Reagan as governor of California, was not able to practice what he preached.

What Figure 5 enables us to see is precisely what we
cannot see in the day-to-day reality of political conflict:
namely, that no political party or ideology expresses the
Truth; the Truth is what we see when we look down from
on high at the entire field of cultural manifestation. What
Figure 5 expresses is a political ecosystem, an ecology of
consciousness in which each biome is necessarily symbiotic
with the other. Something like this way of looking at things
is going to be needed for the survival of human life on earth.

If one wishes to see the dynamics of the four value orientations independent of the color scheme, then the model
permits one simply to detach the four corner triangles to
consider the meanings of the words associated with each
point (see Figure 6).

The Conservative is the mediation of *Cosmos* and *Routine;* the emotional tone associated with this orientation is
agapé, the prayerful love and devotion of the pious man or
woman. The Liberal is the mediation of *Cosmos* and *Charisma,* the established world wed to the power of innovation,
the world of Harvard and M.I.T. The emotional tone associated with this orientation is *logos,* the mental quality of
intellectuality and scientific analysis. The Radical is the
mediation of *Chaos* and *Charisma;* one polarity of his or her
being is pulled toward intellectual innovation and transformation, and the other is pulled toward the ecstasy of total
disruption. The emotional tone associated with this orientation is *eros,* or passion. In the sixties the radicals proposed
some intelligent schemes for social transformation, but their
hearts were more fascinated by the purity of failure (otherwise known as "not selling out") and the need to perish like

kamikaze pilots in the seizure of some great political vision. The net result of the erotic politics of yippie and hippie alike was not a new social order, but a passionate and passing affair with the body politic. It remains to be seen whether the Greens of West Germany will also fail because of this erotic lust for failure as the only true sanctification of ideological purity.

The Radical, as has been often noted before, is not unlike the Reactionary, for one polarity of the Reactionary's being is similarly attracted to *Chaos;* but in his or her own internal contradictions is also the pull toward stability and order, the value of *Routine.* (The Nazis expressed this contradiction to perfection.) For the Reactionary, the resolution of this contradiction is not in visions of sexual ecstasy and transformation, but in death and transfiguration. The Reactionary, whether he is a German Adolph Hitler, an Irish Padraic Pearse, or an Iranian Ayatollah Khomeini, loves to invoke death and sacrifice for the nation. Thus, the emotional tone associated with this orientation is *thanatos* (death). In the Reactionary's desire to return to some imagined ideal past is sounded a note that the world is a fallen place and only in the ultimate return of *thanatos* can the gnostic escape this world of compromise and entrapment in systems of contradiction, ambiguity, and complexity.

Perhaps at this point it would be prudent to emphasize that these models are archetypal but not deterministic; that is, they are descriptive but not proscriptive. The universe is open-ended and free, and the unique always has individual ways to express universal principles. One should not try to reify these principles into concrete forces that physically constrain the individual in a political system. There is a net in the game of volleyball and a set of rules, but the rules and the court are not the game; they are merely conditions that enable the game to come into being. Each game is unique because the universal principles are held in consciousness. This free relationship between unique and universal is part of the play of the universe; it is the basic freedom that enables us to see that life is not a closed machine of units in a system of uniformity. The mystical body of Christ is precisely this *crossing* of the unique with the universal; the Satanic mass of collectivization is the order in which the unit is compelled to be uniform: from the Brown Shirts of Hitler to the red shirts of Rajneesh.

The four value orientations are not deterministic, but they are archetypal in the sense that they express a pattern that recurs in different contexts. Like the four points of the compass, they express organization and direction, but they do not define or control all the individual complexities of landscape and weather that take place. To see this relationship between archetypal and individual, or universal and unique, we can continue to use Egyptian mythology as a philosophical narrative. Osiris is the Liberal, the source of mental innovation as the culture hero who creates agriculture and the arts of civilization. The Reactionary opposed to his new ways is Seth, a figure associated with the flint tools of the Paleolithic past. Isis is the Conservative, the person who literally conserves as she gathers up the pieces of the dismembered Osiris. She is also conservative in the sense that as the new sister-wife she is the transformed image of the old Great Mother Goddess, for it is as a Divine Mother that she gives birth to the son of Osiris, Horus. Horus is the Radical, the radically new: the son of the father who breaks with tradition to displace the authority of the matrilineal mother's brother to establish a new patriarchal lineage.

The four value orientations, or political parties, attempt to play out their values *in* time, but basic to an older esoteric knowledge is the perception that there is a cycle of ages to the seasons of the cosmos, and in each age different values predominate at different times. In Vedic, Egyptian, and Greek mythologies this cycle was seen as a sequence of four ages. The most familiar modern adaptation of this sequence comes from Giambatista Vico's *The New Science,* in which he presents the sequence as: I. Age of Gods; II. Age of Heroes; III. Age of Men; and IV. Age of Chaos. The dynamics of the four ages can be seen as well in the crystal of the Basic Quaternity, as shown in Figure 7.

The Age of Gods is the perfect golden age in which *Logos* and *Agapé* are balanced in *Cosmos.* The Age of Heroes rests on the foundation of *Charisma, Logos,* and *Eros.* The Age of Heroes is not the divine age of union and harmony but of individual assertion of the hero in his display of excellence, his *aresteia.* An archetypal figure of this age is Odysseus, the crafty inventor of the Trojan Horse and the lover of Circe. The Age of Men rests upon *Routine, Agapé,* and *Thanatos;* this is the age of duty, devotion, and sacrifice of the individual hero for the common good, the age of a gentleman of the British Empire who follows the routines of his class to die for his queen in the colonies. The Age of Chaos, the age in which we now live, rests upon the foundation of *Chaos, Eros,* and *Thanatos.* It is an age in which entertainment comes from the linkage of sex and violence in popular movies, an age in which politics is polarized to extremes with revolutionary terrorism at one end and establishment thermonuclear terrorism at the other.

In this mythological way of looking at historical time, the Age of Chaos overlaps with a New Age of Gods, as in *The Last Judgment* of Bosch or the prophecies of Shambala of the Tibetans. Time moves in an alternating rhythm of sudden transformative catastrophes and long periods of steady state in which the innovation is consolidated in an adaptation that can be called a world, or an age. At this level of narrative, mythology and the "punctuated equilibrium" of the evolutionists are analagous.

The crystal of the Basic Quaternity is outside of time, just as the grammar of the English language is outside of time, but these words are read in the serial progression of the world of time; and yet, without the internalized grammar of English, these words would be unrecognizable. So it is with these archetypal systems of patterning. The grammar of a language is at the mental level of synchrony rather than diachrony, but these crystals do not derive from the Mental Plane; they derive from the Causal Plane, the ontological plane of the *Daimon.* If one takes up residence in a foreign country, one can begin to internalize the grammar of the foreign language without conscious study; if one takes up residence in the planes of Being foreign to the ego (generally this is done through meditation), then one can begin to "see" these multidimensional crystals of *Daimonic* awareness. And just as sentences of a language take time, but the grammar does not, so do these crystals seem to unfold in time as their implicate possibilities become actualities. In the performance of universal, archetypal patterns in unique and individual historical circumstances, order and freedom come in to play. As one gazes at the crystal in meditation, one can see that it would take a volume to unpack the implicit meanings, and even when the crystal is dropped into time, it takes time to explain it. Imagine me showing Figure 8 in a lecture hall and then saying, "There, you see. Now we know how to rethink the body politic."

People would think me crazy, for craziness is precisely a problem in communication, not just among human beings, but among the parts of an individual as well. When the paranoid senses *Daimonic* awareness, turns it into imagery, and then takes it literally to rave on about the end of the world or the creatures from beyond the stars in their flying saucers, he is having a communication problem, a problem of language, within the dynamics of his own being and not simply with his fellow human beings.

The Tibetans use many of these crystals as yantras, or meditational diagrams, in their educational systems of visualization, but I believe that these archaic modes of thought are going to return in places where they are least expected: in the world of computer graphics. In the days of Andy Hardy, the United States celebrated the technological superiority of its culture in which each teenager had an automobile; when, in the new California culture, every teenager has a personal computer, new forms of old "right brain" visualizations will be stimulated. I have tried clumsily to give a sense of these crystals with colored chalk on classroom chalkboards and with photographic slides in lecture halls, but imagine a video cassette with music in which these triangles could be presented, not as static, two-dimensional geometry, but as dynamic pulsating topologies. For example, as one showed the four political parties in opposition in the field of action, one could enable the individual to move to a level above the ideology of a single party, capitalist or communist, to see the more complex ecology of consciousness in which human beings live. By holding some of the triangles in black-and-white, while others unfold in color, one could with computer animation make the difficult much simpler. I do believe that in the future, after the physiologically damaging side effects of cathode tubes have been eliminated, computer animation will enable the new Pacific Basin culture to turn on the historical spiral to appreciate ancient hieroglyphic thinking in a new way. As this happens, I would expect that just as the Japanese surprised us with how good they could be with electronic hardware, the Chinese will surprise us in just how good they can be with innovative software and new iconic computer languages.

Because the Basic Quaternity is a universal structure, it can be used to explicate the dynamics of relationships in many different contexts. For example, instead of using the four corner triangles to describe the four political parties, the triangles can be used to describe the four basic political and economic worlds: I. First World-Economy, Communist Nations (the Soviet Union and Eastern Europe); II. Second World-Economy, the Capitalist Industrial Nations (the "Trilateral" United States, Japan, and Western Europe); III. Third World-Economy, the Developing Nations (such as Brazil and the OPEC nations); and IV. Fourth World-Economy, the Least Developed Nations. (See Figure 9.)

The first corner triangle of *Cosmos, Agapé,* and *Routine* expresses communism in its ideal form, free of Stalinism. This is basically an extremely conservative society that holds to the collective good. The second corner triangle of *Cosmos, Logos,* and *Charisma* describes the capitalist world-economy. This is the world that holds to the individual good, to cultural and artistic freedom and license; it is a world of technological innovation, of a restless energy that disrupts the stable and secure order of steady-state societies. In its ideal form, such an American society is dynamic and creative, but in its actuality it is destructive, and both nature and traditional cultures suffer from its uncontrollable energy. The third corner triangle of *Charisma, Eros,* and *Chaos* describes revolutionary Africa. Africa and Latin America are the unstable, revolutionary spaces of the resource-rich and the resource-poor; as such, they hold *Charisma* and *Chaos* in such contradictory tension that they are likely to continue to produce great artists amid a condition of unbearable suffering and world disordering.

The fourth corner triangle is an embodiment of the Reactionary archetype; it is a constellation of the forces of *Routine, Thanatos,* and *Chaos.* Iran and Afghanistan express the resource-rich and the resource-poor polarities of this Reactionary archetype. The Ayatollah Khomeini is the Reactionary archetype *par excellence,* for he is in love with sacrifice and martyrdom. The midnight of death and transfiguration calls to the depths of his soul, and he can see no evil in sending twelve-year-olds into the mined battlefields of Iraq.

The Four World-Economies thus correspond to the four political value orientations. Russia and China are the great conservatives of the world; America and Western Europe are the great liberals; the OPEC nations are the radical upstarts who are challenging the great powers and changing the capitalist world-system overnight; and Iran is the great reactionary seeking to lead a neomedieval Islam into a religious rejection of the secular and technological West. Naturally, these value orientations are dynamic and changing; one minute a country can be under the sway of one archetype (as, under the Shah, Iran was fanatically committed to modernization), and then in the next minute a revolution can take over a country to catch it up in the fervors of nativistic revolt. Revolutionary France flipped over from the Age of Reason to the Reign of Terror; so the archetypal pattern would lead us to suspect that the cliché "opposites attract" is based upon an intuitive insight.

In the present transitional world-system, the interactions of the four world-economies are unconscious, full of projections, and laden with ignorant conflict and violence. As we become more conscious, the four world-economies will be seen as one planetary ecology in which the health of the whole requires that one does not dominate the others. The definitions of the four worlds will then not be economic, as in resource-rich and resource-poor, but probably artistic and scientific.

My purpose in invoking these archaic modes of thought

in a modern context of international relations is to work to make the unconscious conscious: to move out of the mechanisms of a remorseless karma in which we become what we hate into a more enlightened and initiatic awareness of the play of Being. The Basic Quaternity enables us to see and model relationships of a more complex, polycentric, or, at least, quadracentric, variety. Our former model of organization was the circle. There was the center, a London or New York, and there was the periphery, the outlying provincial areas. The center dominated the periphery, and that was that. And when another center rose to challenge the old one, there was conflict and war. Such a mentality leads to the eventual war between New York and Moscow. By suggesting other models of relationship, I am trying to suggest (perhaps naively) that a transition from one world-system to another is possible without World War III.

The Basic Quaternity is exoterically a model of international relations and esoterically a model for the planes of Being within the individual person. Thus the Quaternity is a model of both vertical and horizontal organization: the universe of the planes of Being (Causal, Mental, Astral, and Physical) and the outer world of the economies.

The Basic Quaternity can also be seen as a model of cultural relationships in the field of sports. Now in our culture of war and conflict most of our sports are dyadic: there are two antagonistic teams and two goals, whether we are playing football, hockey, basketball, or volleyball. Since sports, in their historical origins, are stylizations and sublimations of warfare, they are tied up with competition, aggression, and conflict. When our culture has made the shift to nonego in the individuated being that is aware of the *Daimon,* and nonideology in the society that is aware of the ecology, I suspect that our forms of sports will change dramatically. One possible expression of this could be a shift from dyadic to quadratic, as if the Basic Quaternity itself became the court for a tennis or volleyball game in which the teams danced in constantly shifting alliances rather than in permanent teams defined by a single identity of "us versus them."

Now, as the Devil is the ape of God, and there always is a shadow form to manifestation, it is important to anticipate what the shadow form for an enantiomorphic polity would be. My guess would be that it would be one in which the society moves from hot ideologies to cool technologies. The technocrat, too, would like to see a global culture in which ideologies are set aside, but for the engineer the foundations of the new world culture are technique and technology. But either in its Skinnerian form as a behavioral utopia, or in its sociobiological form as the genetically engineered and managed elitist state, these fantasies of power are simply irreligious versions of the collectivization of the unit in the uniform. The archetype of the mystical body of Christ celebrates the food-sharing communion in which the unique and the universal experience unity. The archetype of the demonic body of Satan, whether scientifically or religiously expressed, is one of total control through the annihilation of differences.

In a world-system based upon the shift from ideology to technology, the culture of total control would create a monocrop world-state, to do to the ecology of the world what agribusiness has done to the prairies and the aquifers. In a new world-system based upon the shift from ideology to ecology, the old cultures would not be annihilated, but rather they would be involved in a new context. Nations would become artistic styles rather than economic powers, a transition one can already see taking place in France, for there is no future for France as a world power (though she still dreams of recovering her former glory), but there is a future for France as an intellectual and cultural power. In the formation of the post–World War II world-system, as the Americans played the role of the new Romans, Europe played the role of the old Hellenistic Greeks lending a touch of class to global operations. Now that the shift westward is continuing, and power is moving from the East Coast to the West Coast, New York becomes the old culture lending a little class to the crass operations of Denver, Dallas, Houston, and Los Angeles. Europe becomes the truly ancient civilization, much as India was to Rome in the third century A.D., and although we Westerners do not often know where our astronomy, linguistics, literature, mathematics, and philosophy come from, there is no question that the India of Nagarjuna was more brilliant than Hellenized Egypt or Imperial Rome. As it was for classical India, it may now be for Europe.

In the classical world-system that grew up around the shores of the Mediterranean, Hebrew morality, Greek philosophy, and Roman law became the foundation for the succeeding world-system, the medieval European. In the later Middle Ages, economics, art, and science became the foundation for the modern world-system, the new culture that grew up around the shores of the Atlantic. Now a new world-system is emerging around the shores of the Pacific, and as Eastern mysticism meets Western science, a wholly new Pythagoreanism is being born. As we move from a culture of competition, accumulation, and conflict in industrial civilization to cooperation, sharing, and coevolution in a planetary ecology, we will be taking a step as important in our evolution as the movement from animal to human. No doubt, all through this transformation there will be resurgences of human, all too human, behavior in competition, greedy accumulation, and warfare over critical resources, but, nevertheless, humanity will continue to stagger and stumble along the path illuminated by the longings of the heart and the intuitions of the spirit.

Whether the movement from one world-system to another will involve stumbling or total collapse may well depend on the success or failure of the New Age movement. Now, as we stand poised at the edge of a great transformation, we are prophetically inspired and politically armored as never before. Perhaps the movement from the *mystique* to the *politique* need not be one of degeneration; certainly, faced as we are with the risk of World War III, we have to take the risk of finding, beyond the conventional politics of corruption, the new and surprising politics of incarnation.

Notes

1. The Letters of W. B. Yeats, ed. Allan Wade (London: Rupert-Hart Davis, 1954), p. 922.

2. E. F. Schumacher, A GUIDE FOR THE PERPLEXED (New York: Harper & Row, 1978), p. 127.

3. Henri Atlan, ENTRE LE CRISTAL ET LA FUMÉE (Paris: Seuil, 1979), p. 57.

4. Goethe, *Faust: Part One,* trans. Philip Wayne (London: Penguin, 1958), p. 75.

5. For a more complete analysis of the Isis and Osiris myth, see "Civilization and Initiation in Ancient Egypt" in William Irwin Thompson, THE TIME FALLING BODIES TAKE TO LIGHT (New York: St. Martin's Press, 1981), p. 209.

CHAPTER 3

The Four
Cultural Ecologies
of the West

*A*ll descriptions *of* the past are *in* the present; therefore, history tells our descendants more about us than it does about the imaginary creatures we like to call our ancestors. Like an image before us in the rear-view mirror of a car, the picture of where we have been keeps changing as we move forward in space and time. The narratives of the past from even so short a time ago as the beginning of our own twentieth century now no longer describe us, and so each generation must reinvent the past to make it correspond to its sense of the present.

In much the same way, futurism is little more than a not very imaginative managerial description of the implications of the present. Futurology, like archaeology, is an academic way of closing down the past and the future so that they are no longer open to the imaginative expansion of the present.

The space of the present is under the political control of technocratic management; so it is important that the thought police patrol the exits. With Herman Kahn guarding the year 2000 A.D. and Aubrey Burl guarding the year 2000 B.C., we are closed in and protected from any narrative of future or past that is not propaganda for our present technological mentality.[1]

All of which is only another way of saying that the past and the future do not exist; nevertheless, we need these narrative fictions, for we gain knowledge by looking backward at patterns and forward in anticipation of the results of our actions. We can live without a substantially real past or future, for our materialistic society is more concerned with the immediate demands of the present; it is only when we find that the present doesn't exist absolutely either (for the very act of perceiving it takes away its definition by pushing it into the past) that we become disoriented. When we look down for a ground to our being, we find ourselves walking on water that reflects the sky.

Physics, of all sciences, was the first to deliver us from the illusion of the substantial reality of matter, and it was Heisenberg who pointed out more than two generations ago that we do not live in nature, but in a description of nature.[2] Coeval with Heisenberg's analysis of matter was Heidegger's analysis of being, which revealed the groundlessness of basing being on a metaphysics of substance, on a substantial reality. (Notice that our very word for truth comes from the Latin *res* and means "thing" and "thingishness.")

Politicians like to pretend that these philosophical matters are obscure and the concern only of professors of philosophy, but we have merely to watch the rock music videos of the young to realize that the multiple, interpenetrating spaces of the paintings of Magritte (as, for example, in his *L'enfance d'Icarre*) are now part of the common imagery of videos such as the Cars' "You Might Think I'm Crazy." Computers and video synthesizers have democratized epistemology. In industrial culture there is a Left and a Right, and a top and a bottom; but in electronic culture, top becomes pop, and Left and Right become replaced with the fast forward of Jerry Brown and the rewind of Ronald Reagan.

Music video puts all human emotions into quotation marks, for it is clear that the love song is not expressing love, but is about "love." In the same way, the video imagery of war and apocalypse, whether sweetly sung by Boy George or screamed by Kiss, is not communicating an attraction or a revulsion to war; it is expressing a displacement from history. All history simply becomes quotes from old movies, whether Lang's *Metropolis* or Riefenstahl's *The Triumph of the Will*, and in the displacement of consciousness from literate history to the now of electronic video, the young are doomed to Blake's "dull eternal round." Paris is still an ancient capital of a literate civilization, so the *Bonsoir les clips* of music videos only comes on for twenty minutes at the end of the day's programming. Appropriately enough, the show comes on after the late news, for music video is truly the last news. Ah, but in New York and Toronto, MTV and Much Music run twenty-four hours a day. We may not yet have Nietzsche's Eternal Return, but we do have perpetual reruns.

Top and pop in culture, like past and future in the present, are the limbs of the body politic, and one cannot understand contemporary society merely by reading *The New York Review of Books* or watching MTV. An elite may define a self-conscious approach to culture through a literature, but a cultural ecology is not a literary definition of a social group; it is a tissue of simultaneities of organisms playing out a similar adaptive approach in different contexts, different demes, different biomes. Heidegger may work to destruct metaphysics, and Derrida may follow him in an effort to destruct literary discourse, but *les enfants du rock* defer and displace automatically and unthinkingly, for the effect of putting all emotions into quotation marks in music video is to deconstruct the message with the medium. The *content* of the clips is clearly banal and atrocious, but the content is not what is really going on.

The literary critic and the philosopher analyze a culture from within that culture's definition of culture.[3] The anthropologist, suffering from geographical displacement, labors to define the dynamics of culture from outside but still carries within himself or herself a theory of dynamics and mechanics that he or she has borrowed from early European physics. The cultural ecologist is, like *les enfants du rock,* working from a geographical and a psychological displacement, for he or she is displaced from the content of his or her own culture and from the content of anthropology's instructions on how to behave as a proper scientific anthropologist. Like an astronaut looking down on the earth from on high, or a mystic looking down on the mind from on high in meditation, the cultural ecologist is displaced from the conventional ground of perception. All of this would be extremely esoteric if technology had not democratized the experience, for the effect of personal computers and music video is to put "civilization" into quotation marks.

This shift in sensibility, this transformation of mentality, is a shift from Atlantic, European, industrial civilization to Pacific, planetary, electronic culture. It is not a shift caused by technology, for that kind of narration of linear causation derives from the old industrial habits of thought; it is a shift in consciousness in which top culture and pop culture are synchronously involved in the adaptive play of and within a new cultural ecology. In many ways, the older philosophers and artists of Europe have foreshadowed the very culture in which they would not feel at home.

The groundlessness of being opens up to us in the old-fashioned books of Heidegger and the old-fashioned canvases of Magritte. Different children will spend the family inheritance of Europe in different ways; Ric Ocasek of the Cars will move from canvas to video synthesizer, but Keiji Nishitani, a personal student of Heidegger, will move from metaphysics to zazen to favor the kind of displacement described by Dogen Zenji as "the dropping off of body and mind":

> True equality is not simply a matter of an equality of human rights and the ownership of property. Such equality concerns man as the subject of desires and rights and comes down, in the final analysis, to the self-centered mode of being of man himself. It has yet to depart fundamentally from the principle of self-love. And therein the roots of

discord and strife lie ever concealed. True equality, on the contrary, comes about in what we might call the reciprocal interchange of absolute inequality, such that the self and the other stand simultaneously in the position of absolute master and absolute servant with regard to one another. It is an equality in love.

Only on the field of emptiness does all this become possible. Unless the thoughts and deeds of man one and all be located on such a field, the sorts of problems that beset humanity have no chance of ever really being solved.[4]

In the Kyoto School of Nishitani, the East reconceptualizes the West to show how the ultimate development of materialism leads to nihilism. But it takes no mirror made in Japan to make us see that about ourselves, for we need only turn the pages of a history of Western painting to see the full story. We begin with Giotto, in whose work nature is merely a stage for a religious event, as in the *Flight into Egypt;* we pass on to Brueghel's *Conversion of Saint Paul,* where the religious event is not as large as the horse's behind; and then we continue on to the landscapes of Ruysdael, where the religious event has dropped out of the picture altogether; from there on the thingishness of reality gets very thick, with still lifes of Kauw and the columnar temples of Poussin; but with Claude Lorrain the twilight over the temples becomes more important than the stones, and we begin to pass over matter into the mysteries of perception; and from there on there is no stopping until Monet's cathedrals melt and solid matter disappears into the nihilism of the Rothko Chapel. With the paintings before us, we can literally see what Nishitani is talking about.

The movement from Heidegger to Nishitani is a Pacific Shift in philosophy,[5] but these Pacific Shifts are not limited to philosophy. The movement from Warren McCulloch to Francisco Varela is a Pacific Shift in neurophysiology; in one the doctrine of materialism is negated, and in the other the doctrine of representationism in the nervous system is negated;[6] but in both cases it is the world view of Atlantic civilization that is being set aside.

It is no cultural accident that both the Kyoto School of philosophy and the Santiago School of neurophysiology share a common Pacific orientation and a common invocation of the relevance of Buddhism to postmodernist science. The Pacific has become the new Mediterranean, with a new relationship between religion and science that is as different from Protestantism and industrial science as Pythagoras's synthesis was from Mesopotamian astrology. Nishitani was a personal student of Heidegger, and Varela has been influenced by Heidegger's writings; but both the Japanese philosopher and the Chilean biologist have not been content to rest with Heidegger's late Christian ontology and have pushed on from a vestigial theology into an explicit a theology of Buddhism. The end of the West becomes the ultimate shore of the East.

The works of Heidegger, Nishitani, and Varela are esoteric and read by a few; but the cultural wave that brings the East to the West carries many forms of life, and the California teenager who sits transfixed before the graphics of his personal computer is also participating in the cultural shift from the Protestant ethic and the spirit of capitalism to Zen and the spirit of cybernetics.

One of the most pioneering thinkers in this cultural shift
was Gregory Bateson. As a participant in the Macy Conferences in New York, which brought the pioneers of cybernetics together, Bateson was part of the creation of a new
science. As an anthropologist doing research among schizo-
phrenics who lived outside normal reality, Bateson made the
phrase "double bind" a household word in the vocabulary of
people who had never heard of him. Bateson is important
not only because of his contributions, but also because his
personal journey in the ecology of Mind is also Western
culture's odyssey from Europe to California. He began his
career at St. John's College, Cambridge, but ended his days
as the philosopher of the furthest edges of the European
mentality. In the last years of his life as a regent of the
University of California, he lived at Esalen Institute in Big
Sur; he died at the Zen Center in San Francisco, but he was
neither a leader of encounter groups nor zazen sessions;
he simply liked to haunt edges to observe the movement
across thresholds flash into "the difference that became information."7

The pattern that connects Bateson to Varela, and both
to Buddhism, was the personal pattern of friendship, as well
as the larger cultural pattern of transformation. A fascination with the groundlessness of Buddhism and the intellectual openness of the Pacific world was shared by both
theoreticians of the biology of knowledge. Both saw the
mental habit of the West to be one in which Being is posited
as *a* being and called God; in which process is arrested in
substance and called material reality; and in which Mind is
made into an organism without an environment and called

the self. For both Bateson and Varela, all three of these cultural activities are part of the same process of reification that isolates God from nature, mind from matter, and organism from the environment; and each of these ends up giving us a system of abstractions that we mistake for reality, to the destruction of both culture and nature.

In Bateson's now classic analysis of "The Effects of Conscious Purpose on Human Adaptation," these three mistakes of thinking are seen to be part of the maladaptation of civilization to nature:

> If consciousness has feedback upon the remainder of mind, and if consciousness deals only with a skewed sample of the events of the total mind, then there must exist a *systematic* (i.e., non-random) difference between the conscious views of self and the world, and the true nature of self and the world. Such a difference must distort the processes of adaptation.[8]

Since Bateson delivered that lecture in Austria in 1968, the distortion in the process of adaptation has now progressed to the point of a disruption about to become a catastrophe. As this catastrophe has already begun to become visible in the death of the forests in Europe, this visibility of process is already changing the way we see history in the rear-view mirror. Now it is inappropriate to mark time with monuments to ego, such as Nelson's Column in Trafalgar Square; now the description of civilization is the sequence of infrared photographs from space that show the Mediterranean's progress toward becoming an industrial sewer.

As we look back on the past in our contemporary imagination, we see it as a movement from the Near Eastern Riverine cultural ecology at the edge of the NASA Landsat photograph, to the Mediterranean cultural ecology in the center, and on to the Atlantic cultural ecology of the European era. When we look down from on high with the eye of an astronaut, we cannot see the celebrated effects of egos with names and monuments; we can only see an action analagous to the presence of bacteria in a compost heap or of a mold in a Petri dish: the changes of color for the seas and the forests tell us of the deadly presence of highly toxic human institutions. Where in this collective action is the individual human will? Is the human being simply a catalytic agent secreted by Gaia to transform the subterranean oceans of oil into a moving gas in the earth's atmosphere? Is human consciousness, as Marx would say, a "false consciousness"? Could it be, in a strange blending of Marx and Buddha, that human beings do not, perhaps, cannot, *know* what they are *doing?* Is Lewis Thomas closer to the ecological truth of symbiotic humanity, and that humans are moving toward fusion all the time that they keep mumbling about the self?

The interest that Buddhism holds for scientists like Bateson and Varela begins to make sense. It is not simply a question of the West's discovery of the *groundlessness* of its emphasis on material reality, but also of the enormous growth of suffering in the expansion of industrial society known as economic development. Buddha's is the aboriginal questioning of the relationship between mind and suffering; so it is small wonder that as science approaches the frontiers of mind in cybernetics and neurophysiology, and as industrial society mass-produces human suffering, thinkers at the edge of European culture, such as Bateson, Nishitani, and Varela, would notice the relevance of the past of Buddhism to the future of science and philosophy.

Given the enormity of human suffering we now face in our declining twentieth century, and given the still youthful vigor of science, I think that this relationship between Buddhism and science will be an enduring Pythagorean marriage and not a passing Romantic affair. The relationship between religion and science is so complex and elaborate that only a civilization is complex enough to elaborate it. Just such a new civilization is emerging around the edges of the Pacific, and the reason that we can look back now to the past and see a movement from Riverine to Mediterranean to Atlantic is precisely because the West is now passing out of the Atlantic cultural ecology of Europe into the new cultural ecology of the Pacific.

The historical movement from one cultural ecology to another can be centuries long, as in the movement from Mesopotamian to classical to medieval; or it can be the journey of a lifetime, as in Bateson's movement from England to California; or it can become a metanoia in which the world is experienced by the individual in an instant. To appreciate the movement out of the old cultural ecology into the new one, consider the experience of the astronaut Russell Schweickart, the first man to float in space without a vehicle to frame his perceptions. Because of a malfunction with his camera, Schweickart had a moment to *be* and not to *do;* in that instant he dropped the linear perspective of the box of his camera to comprehend the earth with his whole body and soul. In his remarks at Lindisfarne, Southampton, in 1974, Schweickart described the experience in the following way:

> You look down there and you can't imagine how many borders and boundaries you cross, again and again and again. And you don't even see them. There you are—hundreds of people in the Mideast killing each other over some imaginary line that you can't see—and from where you see it, the thing is a whole, and it's so beautiful. You wish you could take one in each hand, one from each side in the various conflicts, and say, "Look! Look at that! What's important?"[9]

The world of industrial man is a world of *objects* separated by lines: mansions at one end, dioxin dumps at the other. But in the Pacific-Aerospace cultural ecology, the world is known to be a field of interpenetrating *presences*, and in the world of space one is constrained to be on more intimate terms with one's waste. This is a knowledge that is brought back to earth, for aerospace technologies lead directly to new understandings of ecology. With satellites one sees the life of rivers and seas; with space capsules and shuttles one learns the placing of exhalation and excretion.

Ideologies are excretions of the mind; they are the exhausted remains of once living ideas. They, too, must be put safely to the side as toxic wastes that can kill if they are inappropriately taken in as life-giving food. For Rusty Schweickart, looking down on the violent Middle East, the movement into space became a shift from the ideologies of "us and them" to the ecology of consciousness in which opposites are understood in an involvement of "each in all." The furthest development of industrial technology and its extension into space brings about a rather classic enantio-dromia in which technology triggers a mystical change in consciousness in which an *object* becomes a *presence*, but it also brings about a cultural condition in which the spiritual unconscious, or Gaia, is precipitated into consciousness.

As Bateson has shown, most of Mind is, and must be by definition, inaccessible to consciousness,[10] but how we designate the unconscious is part of the history of consciousness, part of that image in the rear-view mirror that tells us where we have been. Looking back over the twentieth century, we can now see that the uncovering of the unconscious has moved through four stages. First came the uncovering of the instinctive unconscious with Freud; this was essentially a revelation of *eros* and *thanatos* in the basic animal life. Then came the uncovering of the psychic unconscious, the collective unconscious, through the work of Jung. This was a revelation of the archetypes of the emotional life of the soul. Then came the uncovering of the intellectual unconscious, the "positive unconscious" in the work of Lévi-Strauss and Foucault. For the structural anthropologist, mythologies and the sexual life of preliterate humanity expressed patterns that were invisible to the savage but perceived by the ethnologist. For the cultural historian of civilization, like Foucault, the *episteme* of an age was the hidden structure of the mind, the intellectual unconscious, that held economics, linguistics, and art into a relationship not seen by the people of their own era.[11] Bateson's analysis of the ecology of Mind is the transition from the uncovering of the intellectual unconscious to the precipitation of the spiritual unconscious. This revelation takes two forms: first, the unconscious becomes experienced as the body not identified with and hitherto seen as "the other," namely, the environment; and second, the environmentally compressed social consciousness integrates from the threat of crisis to precipitate, not a literate civilization, but a collective consciousness. Another word for revelation is apocalypse, but this mythic narrative of the end of the world should not be taken literally in a paranoid fashion, and should be recognized as expressing not annihilation but the ending of a single world.

Catastrophe literally means "turning over." When one turns over compost with a shovel, one is creating a catastrophe for the anaerobic bacteria in the pile. Wars can be the turning over of civilizations, but for humans with a more ecological awareness, the transition from civilization to planetary culture could be more subtle, unimaginable, and so gradual that, though individuals in various ages intuit the transition and express it in art and paranoid utterance, the transition itself, the turning over, does not take place *in* time until it is finished. Perhaps, the transition from civilization to planetary culture is like the transition from Paleolithic to Neolithic, and the artists who sensed the end of that era said farewell to it in Lascaux and Altamira. For the artist, nothing is the same; for the common man, nothing has changed. Perhaps this is what Yeats meant when he said, "All life is waiting for an event that never happens."

And yet something happened to Rusty Schweickart, and something happened to our world when we saw it from space. Perhaps there is a logarithmic progression to the rate of change, and what a few intuit at the time of Hieronymus

Bosch becomes more widely seen as the discontinuity between the rate of change and the rate of adaptation becomes more dramatic. Certainly with the rapid death of the forests and vineyards in Europe, and with overpopulated Mexico about to become to the United States in 1987 what Ireland was to England in 1845, the world does seem to be a place where culture and ecology are disastrously maladapted to one another.

The samsaric creatures who distort the process of adaptation with conscious purpose do not seem to know what they are doing. When the West Germans created the "economic miracle," they did not know that they were killing the forests. When the city fathers of Los Angeles connived with General Motors to eliminate the Pacific Electric public train system in order to build the freeways, they thought they were making something called "progress." This mistake seems to be as old as civilization itself, for in ancient Uruk, Gilgamesh and Enkidu thought that the right way to go out and make a name for themselves was to slay the spirit of the forest. Civilized humanity will continue to make progress in this way, whether it makes DDT, or plutonium, or thalidomide, or dioxin, or a genetically engineered bacterium with which to spray fruit trees in order to retard the damage to agribusiness from frost.

Conscious purpose derives from conscious identity. As this Western industrial civilization of ours reaches its grand climactic finale, it is timely for us to look back and ask ourselves: Who is this *we?* What is this story we keep telling ourselves about *Western* science, and *Western* technology, and *Western* humanistic values?

This narrative of identity in which we take our being marks time with various monuments and builds its pantheons to celebrate the nation's great, but if we move our eyes up from the level of the streets of Paris or London, we do not see people or their monuments any longer. The samsaric creatures who thought that they were separate from nature when they dug wells and chopped down trees do not show up in the picture, except at the end of the story as the changing colors of a dying Mediterranean. As we look down on the stage for their story, we see a mold called civilization spread from river to sea to ocean. We do not see tribes, peoples, or nations, but we do see four distinct ecologies affected by human culture; so, that is why I prefer to call these configurations "cultural ecologies" and look back at the narrative of "Western civilization" to see it as a cumulative movement through four stages.

The first cultural ecology of the West was the Riverine, that lattice of city-states spread between the Tigris and the Euphrates in the fourth millennium B.C. This historic transformation of Neolithic villages and towns into cities was not simply an expression of an increase in population, but a reorganization of the structure of society. This systematic transformation involved new forms of communication in the appearance of writing, new forms of technology in the appearance of plows and irrigation works, and new institutions in the forms of standing armies and elevated temples. We now look back in identification with this complex and call it "civilization" to see ourselves in it.

Neolithic gathering and gardening were attuned to local conditions and limits. There were no great irrigation systems to transform the marshes of gatherers into the fields of farmers. Civilization, by contrast, was an extensive alteration of the landscape, and the dikes and canals of the irrigation works contributed greatly to the salinization of the soil.

The salinization of the soil is civilization's first form of pollution, and it tells us right at the start something very important about the structural organization of civilization: namely, that pollution is not a random noise or static that clings to the transmission of the signal as consciousness passes through the medium of nature, but, rather, it is itself a communication, albeit an unconscious one. It is not random, but a systematic description of the form of the disruption; it is like a shadow that describes the form of an object's intrusion into the light. It is not noise precisely because it is a signal; but because it is not recognized to be information, it cannot be classed as an ordinary signal. So, let us say that it is dissonance rather than noise, for dissonance derives from cultural conventions of tuning. Dissonance can contribute to background noise as long as it remains unconscious and unrecognized, but if the dissonance becomes interesting enough to attract awareness, and thus is pulled out of the unconscious into the creative play of mind, then dissonance becomes recognized as a signal.

Pollution, then, like a neurotic symptom, is a form of communication. To ignore the symptom, to thrust it to the side of awareness and push it back into the collective unconscious, is to perform the same action that created the pollution, the dissonance, the neurotic symptom, in the first place. The end result of ignoring the communication is to stimulate it to the point that the dissonance becomes so loud that it drowns out all other signals. Ultimately, the ignored and unconscious precipitates itself as the ultimate shadow of civilization, annihilation. This is another way of expressing what I have noted before: "If you do not create your destiny, you will have your fate inflicted upon you."[12] The creation of destiny, then, depends on maintaining a more permeable membrane between noise and information, unconscious and conscious, nature and culture.

Civilization, however, is not surrounded by a light, permeable membrane, but a wall, and the intensification of consciousness in writing only contributes to the ignored accumulations of the unconscious. The salinization of the soil was not seen or heard. A local technology, defined by the city's limits, created a problem area larger than its political area of control. And so the very attempt at control through irrigation only created a larger area of the uncontrollable. It would seem that nature has its own homoestatic mechanisms of order that use disorder, and any cultural attempt to control an area rationally only seems to generate a shadow that has the ability to eat the form until it disappears in the light. We call nature wild with good reason, but the fascinating aspect of the cultural patterning of urban civilization is that the problem or crisis, the dissonance, can itself be read as the signal of emergence of the next level of historical order.

It can, that is, be read as a signal by the historian, because what is unconscious for the society is information for the historian precisely because he or she is not *in* its time. So it is that one culture's noise and dissonance can be the succeeding culture's information.

The Mediterranean cultural-ecology followed the Riverine. In the expansion of city-state to empire, political areas strained to become coextensive with their resource areas, if not their ecosystems. In urban civilization a center-periphery dynamic was established in which power was at the center with the literate elite, but the resources were at the periphery with the illiterate provincials. And so soil loss at the center could be offset by importing foodstuffs and materials from the periphery. But as the extension of empire from river to sea took place, deforestation appeared as the price for creating large fleets.

Soil loss can be seen to be a local problem remedied by importing food, but deforestation is not simply the removal of an object; it results in an alteration of the climate over a large area. But here again we see the pattern that the appearance of a crisis can be read, not simply as noise picked up by the signal in transmission through a medium, but as the signal of emergence of the next level of historical order. Removal of a forest creates an atmospheric disturbance. And here again we see that as the area of conscious control is extended, the area of unconscious unmanageability also expands. The human crisis comes as the political area and the ecosystem are not coextensive. (By definition, conscious purpose and the larger "ecology of Mind" can never be congruent.) Nature has built-in defenses against rationalization, because total management would shut down spontaneity, novelty, and change; therefore, the defense is a tissue of contradictions. Disorder is homeostatic; the capacity for innovation is held through forms of maintenance that involve noise, randomness, and catastrophes used as stochastic mechanisms. The shape of nature is a form for which we have no topological mapping. It is a form of opposites: order and disorder, steady state and catastrophe, pattern and randomness, continuity and innovation. The ultimate enantiomorphic polity is Gaia herself.

The third cultural ecology is oceanic, specifically Atlantic. We know this formation under the more familiar designation of industrial civilization. The technology is one of steam and internal combustion, and this gaseous, thermodynamic activity is poetically appropriate,[13] for the environmental disturbance is not merely one of soil loss or local deforestation, but of global atmospheric change. These are the changes that we, who come at the end of industrial civilization, can see in the forms of acid rain and the Greenhouse Effect. Once again, the political area is not coextensive with the ecosystem, though the British certainly strained to make it so in the nineteenth century; and, once again, we can see that the crisis indicates the emergence of the next level of historical order, for the atmospheric damage indicates a movement in cultural activity from the oceanic to the planetary.

The fourth cultural ecology is space; its human foundation, however, is the Pacific Basin. In the cultural relationships between Japan and California, one can observe the technological shift from matter to information, from the old European civilization spread out from London and Paris to New York, to the new Pacific Basin civilization spread out from Los Angeles and Tokyo to Sydney.

Although this new culture is focused on the Pacific Basin,

the global quality of the fourth cultural ecology is expressed in the fact that there is not simply one crisis, but an accumulation of all the preceding crises. We encounter salinization and soil loss in the United States from the use of center-pivot irrigation and the mining of fossil water. We encounter sudden and massive deforestation in Latin America and Indonesia, and when these are added to atmospheric changes from industrial pollution, we encounter not simply localized disturbances, but alterations of global weather patterns. And as the forests die or are cut down, this loss of soil and water table accelerates the rate of change in weather patterns. Whether all of these will result in the advent of a new ice age or the melting of the ice caps and the flooding of coastal cities such as New York, or both in succession, is now being debated by scientists.

When we look back over the pattern of development from Riverine to Mediterranean to Atlantic to Pacific-Aerospace, we can see that Western civilization is correct in its identification with the urban revolution of the fourth millennium b.c., for the story is *our* story, and not one of the environmental problems of civilization has been "solved" since 3500 b.c. The problems were simply deferred by moving into a new cultural ecology. But now we have come full circle, and all the problems are accumulating in what can only be described as the climax of civilization itself.

The human response to this climactic crisis has been Janus-headed; one face looks for a way out through an imagination of the past, the other through an imagination of the future. The celebrators of hunting and gathering as an ecologically balanced culture, such as the poet Gary Snyder, tend to see civilization as a pathology. The celebrators of technology, such as the physicist Gerard O'Neill, see nature as the wrong vehicle for culture and have proposed space colonies as the proper medium in which technology can grow independent of the constraints of an earthly ecology. Both reactions to the present are literally reactionary. Hunters and gatherers are not innocent, and the extinction of the Pleistocene megafauna can be blamed on their techniques of using prairie fires and stampedes to eliminate whole species in their hunts. Civilization, if it is pathological, simply makes the pathology of human culture more visible. The task is not to eliminate humanity in a romantic celebration of nature, or to eliminate nature in a romantic celebration of technology, but to understand the enantiomorphic dynamism of that oxymoron *human nature*. The planetary ecological crisis allows us to see for the first time the nature of a planetary ecology. If we can begin to understand the pattern that connects noise to innovation, catastrophe to selection, nature to culture, we have the possibility of becoming alive in vitally more imaginative ways than in the male-bonded clubbiness of the hunting camp or the space colony.

From the beginning of civilization there have been wild slippages in nature that have always kept it out of the control of culture. Heisenberg's Indeterminacy Principle is not simply a narrative limited to quantum mechanics; it is a narrative of the limits of the mappings of observation: if you can fix a society's location, you cannot fix its ecological momentum. Bateson saw the discrepancy between conscious purpose and the larger pathways outside the body in the ecology of Mind as a form of disharmony that resulted in crises of maladaptation; but perhaps the relationship is more basic than that, more a question of ontology than epistemology. Perhaps *knowing* can never become identical with *being*, or perhaps it can only with the achievement of Buddhist Enlightenment.

The Christian poet Robert Browning said that "a man's reach should exceed his grasp, else what's a heaven for?" Since we have no historical evidence of the presence of Enlightened societies, for even the Taoist monks used charcoal to make the ink with which they made their celebrated paintings of nature,[14] we can assume that the slippage of nature out of humanity's grasp has to do with a fundamental slippage of being from knowing. Like a shadow that does not permit us to jump over it, but moves with us to maintain its proper distance, pollution is nature's answer to culture. When we have learned to recycle pollution into potent information, we will have passed over completely into the new cultural ecology.

Although nature has her built-in protections against the schemes of total control that would, in effect, be totalitarian, human beings cannot refrain from the impulse to extend their control. Each time that Western civilization did expand, it struggled to internalize the preceding cultural ecology, and it strained its reach to extend its grasp in a political control up to the margins of the new cultural ecology. Mediterranean culture internalized the Riverine, and Roman society strained to turn the Mediterranean area into an empire. The English internalized the Mediterranean (that is

what Nelson's Column celebrates) and strained to turn their
new oceanic cultural ecology into the British Empire.

Compelling as the idea of empire may be for some people,
in the words of Bishop Berkeley's rejection of scientific
materialism, "We Irish think otherwise." The idea of empire is a poor abstraction of a living process; it is a crude
oversimplification of an ecology, and perhaps this is why life
always defeats empire *in* time. The historian of the modern
world-system, Immanuel Wallerstein, sees the expansion of
the West as an ambivalence, even an oscillation, in the
application of two forms of political activity. One he characterizes as that of a world empire, the other that of a world
economy.[15] The current struggles between the United
States of America and the Soviet Union can be seen, therefore, to be not so much a conflict between capitalism and
communism (the contents of their structures), but between
a modernizing and deracinating world economy that puts
McDonald's hamburgers in Paris and Disneyland in Tokyo,
and a traditional and very conservative form of world empire
that seeks to define the periphery in terms of the single
center of Moscow.

One can therefore say that an empire is an abstraction of
an ecosystem, that an economy is a shadow form of an
ecology, and that what human beings are now struggling to
create is a healthier cultural ecology in which pollution,
noise, and dissonance are understood.

The United States has a high tolerance for noise, but is
actually a fairly homogeneous culture; Western Europe has
a lower tolerance for noise, but is highly heterogeneous.
Given the double presence of noise and heterogeneity, it is

difficult to imagine that the Soviet Union could swallow up Western Europe. The imperial way of dealing with noise and dissonance is simply to suppress them. The economic way of dealing with them is to circulate them through society and make a profit from the movement across thresholds. One cultural system places a high value on stability and sees the steady state as the natural condition; the other places a high value on innovation and sees change as the natural condition. Europe is the unstable shore between the world economy of the Americans and the world empire of the Russians, and so its instability makes it rather unpredictable. But its very instability does argue that it is no more open to conquest by the Russians than Latin America is to conquest by the *gringos*. America's fear of Soviet expansion is a projection that is a caricature of its own military expansion into Puerto Rico and Hawaii. Reagan's fear of communist world domination is Manifest Destiny in a Hollywood projection in which the reversed image is righted by the lens that has cleverly hidden the inversion of reality.

The season of cultural florescence is, by its very nature, transitory. The Dutch were world leaders in commerce, art, and science in the seventeenth century, and then they lost their leadership to the English in the eighteenth century. The English, in turn, lost their role to the Americans in the twentieth century. Now some Europeans, including Johan Galtung of the Oslo Peace Institute, think that the Americans will lose their leadership to the Japanese. The Americans, for their part, are afraid that the twenty-first century could see Japanese momentum added to Chinese mass to create an unstoppable Asian velocity into the future. But in truth the Americans are happy to have the Japanese to compete with in the race for the supercomputer, for Americans need a Super Bowl to spur them on. The Japanese are not likely to overtake the Americans, for their primary and secondary educational systems tend to crush the young and kill any sense of risk taking, imagination, spontaneity, and play. American high schools, by contrast, are a joke, but as kids tinker with computers, as once they tinkered with customizing cars, they are free to grow in the more relaxed ways that lead to such mythic stories as the creation of Apple Computer. Easy high schools and encouraging universities are the secret of American success. Given its Stanfords, Cal Techs, M.I.T.'s, Berkeleys, Swarthmores, and Amhersts, America is not yet into decline, but is, in fact, entering a period of cultural transformation greater even than the Industrial Revolution that passed over Great Britain in the eighteenth century.

If we were simply shifting the center of world-power from one world-city to another, "history" would be the same old story of rise and fall; however, because we are moving out of one cultural-ecology into another, history is unpredictable, but not unimaginable. The larger patterns of historical development can often help us to see what is forming seemingly local events, much in the same way that geology can help us to see what forces formed our local hills and streams; but one of the more interesting patterns of the perception of historical development is to notice the way in which different narratives become isomorphic. The four cultural ecologies that I have chosen line up in an interesting way with the typologies of both Marx and McLuhan. One chose systems of production and distribution, the other systems of communication; but the shift from one form to another was also synchronous with a reorganization of cultural ecologies, as we can see below:

Cultural Ecology	Economy	Communication System
Riverine	Asiatic	Script
Mediterranean	Feudal	Alphabetic
Atlantic	Capitalistic	Print
Pacific-Space	Socialistic	Electronic

Because Marx was writing in the middle of the Industrial Revolution, he overemphasized technology and the means of production, for, in large measure, he was also reacting to what he felt was the excessive idealism of the Hegelian school. Marx had no way of anticipating the shift from hardware to software, and he had little chance to see that capitalism's emphasis on innovation would carry it from one culture into another and that Russia's revolution would lock its grip onto the industrial mentality. McLuhan had the advantage of coming right in the middle of the shift from print to electronics, and he had the advantage of the perspective that comes from sitting to the side of history. Marx was in the center of the industrial mentality in London; McLuhan, however, was not in Los Angeles, but Toronto, and Toronto, like a fly in amber, is a beautiful fossil of the Scot's vision of the Protestant ethic and the spirit of capitalism. McLuhan disliked change and innovation, but in his fascination with the culture he studied, he spoke for the ambivalence of most Ontarians. Nevertheless, McLuhan saw what most Americans could not, and that was themselves. His analyses of the sixties make even more sense in the eighties.

As we consider the pattern that connects Marx's means of production to McLuhan's system of communication, we can notice that each shift from one to the other tended to introduce a new form of polity.

Cultural Ecology	Polity
Riverine	City-state
Mediterranean	Empire
Atlantic	Industrial nation-state
Pacific-Space	Enantiomorphic?

The kind of polity that is emerging in our epoch is, of course, anybody's guess. The Russians would like to see world communism with Lenin as its prophet and Moscow as its Mecca. The Americans would like to see a global marketplace with minimal national interference in the way of environmental protection or tariffs. I hope that we will have neither a Russian nor an American world-state, but that through the cultural integrations brought on by both the electronic technologies and the ecologies of Mind, we will be able to come up with something more like a planetary cultural ecology in which difference is vital as the information that spells transformation.

Because the eighteenth-century Industrial Revolution turned technology into a form of idolatry, most contemporary political scientists tend to see only technology and economics as expressions of political reality. Pure science, art, and a spirituality that is not religiously institutional are not taken seriously. Fortunately, the French have made up for the Comtian positivism that they foisted on the world, for now cultural historians such as Foucault and Serres look beyond technology for the implicit configuration, the syntax of thought, that is common to the narratives of myth and science. Now, finally, postindustrial humanity is beginning to realize that in spite of Lévi-Strauss, we never can have a science of myth (since our being is always more than our knowing) but that we will always have changing myths of science.

Foucault introduced the concept of *episteme* as the hidden system of coherence in the positive unconscious of an era. Michel Serres has looked at the origins of geometry and noticed the mythic patterns that unite literature and science.[16] Following these insights, and relating them to my own previous discussions of the narratives common to myth and science, I would like to propose a further elaboration of the fourfold typology of cultural ecologies to consider: (1) the dominant form of mathematical articulation, (2) the climactic literary masterpiece, and (3) the dominant mode of religious experience.

Let us begin with the forms of mathematical articulation. Because I am mathematically illiterate, I see patterns precisely because I am outside the content. Like an illiterate peasant who yet has some skill in painting complex patterns on pottery, and who, when he comes upon Sanskrit, Chinese, Arabic, or Greek for the first time, *sees* them as patterns of identity, I look at mathematics as a cultural description. In each of the four cultural ecologies, the processes that have absorbed attention have been quite distinct. It is definitely not the case that there is one universal human nature with four different cultural styles of asking the same questions about the eternal verities. The pattern I see is the following:

Cultural Ecology	*Mathematical Mode*
Riverine	Enumeration
Mediterranean	Geometrizing
Atlantic	Notations of movement, dynamics
Pacific-Space	Catastrophe theory—topology
	(My hunch is that processual, multidimensional morphologies will lead to a return of hieroglyphic thinking of a new sort: a turn on the spiral to a new form of Egyptian science, not Greek abstraction.)

The beginning of mathematics, according to Whitehead, was in the recognition of set and periodicity. The first hunter who observed that three fish and three bears were both instances of threeness took the first step toward the observation of periodicity. Elsewhere I have argued at greater length that the first observations of periodicity had to have been involved with the menstrual cycle and that the primordial mathematician was probably not a hunter, but a gatherer. The Paleolithic stick of computation, christened *le baton de commandement* by the Abbé Breuil, was probably no such male thing at all, but rather a midwife's tally stick for the lunar calender of "women's mysteries."[17] Menstruation and mensuration are related, and the lunar cosmologies that Alexander Thom has shown to be expressed in the megalithic stone circles of Britain speak of a cosmology that is not military, masculine, and Bronze Age.[18]

The observation of periodicity in woman and moon establishes a mentality that becomes developed in the Paleolithic systems of knowledge in midwifery and some form of lunar astrology. But enumeration is not simply counting; it is relating. Therefore the recital of the relationships of humans and animals, of offspring and parents, is a form of relating humans to a cosmology. Relating genealogy is relating the individual to the class, and it is so important and valued a form of organizing the universe that the mentality of enumeration survives up into the historic period. The enumeration of all the *me's* taken by the goddess Inanna from Eridu to Erech is one of the earliest recorded performances of this mentality, but, so basic is it, that it survives from the Riverine up into the foundations of the Mediterranean epoch. In the catalogue of the ships in Book Two of the *Iliad*, in the recital of the shades who come forth to speak with Odysseus in Book Eleven of the *Odyssey*, and in the recital of the lineages of the gods in Hesiod's *Theogony*, we have three classical performances of the world view implicitly organized by the mentality of enumeration.

To appreciate just what a transformation of world view it is to move from enumerating to geometrizing, we have only to compare the mentality of Hesiod with Pythagoras or Plato. Enumeration is a fairly straightforward way of relating humanity to divinity, but when the line folds into triangles and squares, the pattern becomes more complex. One can begin to see the unconscious emergence of the geometrizing mentality in the *Iliad*, for there the lines of descent are beginning to cross over to create patterns. Leda and Tyndareus give birth to the twins Castor and Clytaemnestra; Leda and Zeus give birth to the twins Helen and Pollux. Then the two sets of twins cross, and Castor and Pollux are raised up into heaven; but Clytaemnestra and Helen remain on earth to become the sources of *eros* and *thanatos* in the world of passionate conflict. When, from another line of descent from Zeus, through Tantalus and Atreus, the brothers Agamemnon and Menelaus are wed to Clytaemnestra and Helen respectively, the lines of descent create the outlines of the battlefield of Troy.

When the line becomes the outline of a form, the metaphor that begins to obsess the ancient imagination is the wall, for the wall is the line seen as container. The *Gilgamesh Epic* opens and closes with a celebration of the wall of the city of Uruk. Book Twelve of the *Iliad* focuses on the wall the Greeks build to protect their invading ships. The wall is the limit, but when Patroclus dares to go beyond the limit, and when he dares to go beyond the limits of his own identity by putting on the armor of Achilles, he is cut down. With the concept of the limit, the mentality of enumeration begins to pass over into the mentality of geometry, for the limit is the form of a thing's existence in time as well as space. In the first thirty-three lines of Book Twelve, Homer explores the idea of the wall as a limit of the Greeks' presence in Troy, the limit of the length of time of Achilles's anger, and the limit of duration against entropy. The forces of chaos raging at the edges of order are personified as the gods Poseidon and Apollo, who take counsel together on how to destroy the wall through the eroding force of rivers, but it is clear that what is being described through gods and immortal spirits of rivers are the ideas of entropy and order.

A genius such as Homer, possessed by his *Daimon*, maintains a permeable membrane between unconscious and conscious, and his ideas have such power because they are neither unconscious nor overrationalized. In that vibrant state they provide vital material for thought for generations to come, for when Thucydides portrays the Athenian fleet of Alcibiades proudly sailing off to disaster at Syracuse, he is performing the idea of Patroclus donning the armor of Achilles to go beyond the limit to his destruction; and when Anaximander explores the idea of the edge of things, the wall of definition that separates the limited from the nonlimited, he, too, is making explicit what was poetically expressed by Homer in Book Twelve:

> The Non-Limited is the original material of existing things; further, the source from which things derive their existence is also that to which they return at their destruction, according to necessity; for they give justice and make reparation to one another for their injustice, according to the arrangement of Time.[19]

The wall is the archetypal image of the limit, the edge between life and death, civilization and savagery, and the poetic metaphor of the wall marks the transition in the cultural evolution of consciousness from the mentality of enumerating to geometrizing. In the Babylonian creation myth, the *Enuma Elish* (circa 1000 B.C.), Ea puts a magic circle around the younger gods to protect them from the god of the underground water, Apsu. The older gods are rest-loving, but the younger gods throw noisy parties, and so the Great Mother of the saltwaters wishes to destroy them to return to her primordial rest. The thermodynamic activity of the youthful and newly emergent gods disturbs the condition of rest and entropy preferred by the Great Mother, and so the battle of the male god, Marduk, is no longer the old Neolithic cosmology of the male as the symbol of vanishing and the female as the symbol of continuity; it is a battle of form versus entropy, of civilized, military patriarchy versus prehistoric matriarchy, of the enduring and the changeless versus transformation. All the ideas that we have since rearticulated into the Second Law of Thermodynamics have their origin in this matrix of myth.

The *Enuma Elish* and the *Iliad* are profound milestones in the cultural evolution of consciousness, for they sum up and finish an ancient mentality at the same time that they announce the mentality to come. In Hesiod's *Theogony* and in Homer's *Iliad*, the mentality of enumeration is consummated and finished. Homer brings us up to the edge of the geometrizing mentality, but it will be the work of Pythagoras and Plato to transform mythology into mathematics. And although C. M. Cornford taught us to see that transformation as the great rational leap "From Religion to Philosophy," we now can see what a mixed blessing abstraction is. Homer remains the greater genius, for he understood and expressed in a way that no subsequent writer has surpassed, the violations of order.

Throughout the Mediterranean epoch, this geometrizing mentality is dominant, both in its medieval Christian elaborations and in its Islamic variations that replace iconography with geometry. Perhaps the supreme expression of this geometrizing world view is in the circles of Dante's *Paradiso,* for at that peak of ecstatic visionary elaboration, Mediterranean humanity can go no further. The revolution for modern humanity will be to clear the landscape by calling all into doubt, and Descartes will sweep his mind clean of medieval geometries to create the grid against which to perceive Galileo's falling bodies.

From analytic geometry to calculus, the genius of modern humanity is focused, not on the static objects held in the geometry of a Platonic ideal realm, but on the dynamics of movement. Plato's circles become Kepler's ellipses. Motion, the narrative that was so inconceivable for Zeno, becomes the beloved of Galileo, Kepler, and Newton. For a few centuries, the notations of movement focus on billiard balls moving in a black space; but in the nineteenth century movement becomes generalized into process, and both thermodynamics and evolution extend the mentality into transformations.

Transformations, of course, bring one to the edge of conventional dimensions, and as the narratives of quantum mechanics flirt with objects of perception that can never be seen but only imagined, human beings begin to realize that there is more to consciousness than objects of perception held in three dimensions.

The end of modernism comes with the multidimensional

topologies of mathematics and physics. At first this finish to modernism is elitist and experienced by only a few physicists like Heisenberg or poets like Yeats, but the rise of electronic forms of communication in our generation has democratized this change of mentality. With the ability to express complex geometries in cathode tubes, computer graphics is beginning to stimulate the processes of visual thinking. There was only so much one could do with chalkboard and chalk, or pencil and paper, but now combinations of music and computer graphics begin to permit new forms of play with multidimensional topologies and ancient yantras. As these forms begin to dance in the imagination, they conspire against materialism by whispering in the scientist's ear, "All this is disguised autobiography, for these crystals are the intelligible bodies of angels and the soul." Like the slave in Plato's *Meno*, who could reason geometrically because of anamnesis, postmodern humans discover mysteries of consciousness where they least expect them.

Even so groping a comparison of mathematical modes of articulation and literary modes of narrative shows us that Lord Snow's famous remark about the "two cultures" of the sciences and the humanities is not helpful in understanding history. Mathematics is relating, genealogy is the logic of one's relations; and both are performances of narrative.

Narrative itself is a human response to time, for it is an attempt to escape the infinity of the present as duration by reifying time into a past. *Ex-isting* means "standing out," "arising out of the indeterminate," or "setting up." Consciousness without an object, without either a sensory construction or a spatial-temporal horizon, would be so maddeningly disorienting as to constitute a condition of absolute terror. Our response to this terror would be to project immediately a spatial-temporal horizon, to project a world.

Something like this consciousness without an object happens every night in dreamless sleep, but since the ego is not there to get in the way with its interpretation of terror, the experience is not remembered. Upon slipping out of this state of undifferentiated Being (described as returning to Brahman in the *Upanishads*), consciousness gathers like a dust cloud collecting in density, and dreams begin to project the world of psyche, that shore between the ocean of Being and the island of the ego. Consciousness becomes so enamored with these projections that its attention becomes fixed, and it wakes up into the projection. First consciousness fixes itself in the psychic world, then it falls asleep and dreams what are memories of the psychic experiences, and then it wakes up into the world of the ego to remember the dreams that themselves are memories of psychic experiences. If consciousness were to move without a transition from the fixed attention of the ego to the undifferentiated Being, it would be interpreted as an experience of terror, a death. But this kind of conscious dying, this mystic death, is precisely what the practioners of meditation strive for. Saint Paul said, "I die daily." But the experience of conscious dying is not exclusively a Christian crucifixion, for students of zazen are awakened at four in the morning so that meditation can begin to wear away the membrane between sleeping and waking, and so that as one is awake in one's dreams and dreaming while meditating, the background to consciousness becomes the foreground as all horizons drop and the ground becomes an open space.

Existence is literally a setup, and so our mathematical and literary narratives are repetition compulsions that move back and forth across the threshold of the infinitely extended present. We do the same thing when we scratch an itch or make love: back and forth across the sensitive spot, touching and withdrawing, to enjoy the sense of difference that is, as Bateson told us, the experience of information. Narratives leave the present to touch the present, to explain it, to know it. And whether the narratives say f =ma, or e=mc^2, or "In the beginning was the Word," they go back and forth across the erotic threshold that separates eternity and time.

And so narratives are not merely *about* time, they are performances *of* time: incarnations in miniature that seek to re-mind us literally. As the bard performs his story, so the mind performs its story, the ego. Since the tongue cannot taste itself and the being cannot know itself, we must come at things through reflection and indirection. We tell stories, but the stories are not always directly about what they tell. Hesiod's *Theogony*, that great climactic work of the mentality of enumeration, is about the evolution of Mind, from the indeterminate, through the psychic realm of gods, and down to the most limited incarnation, the shepherd poet himself.

All narratives, whether they are artistic, religious, or scientific, are at their deepest level disguised autobiographies of the human race. At the level of the root idea, the *Enuma Elish* and the Second Law of Thermodynamics are mythopoeic. And when science tells us who we are, where we come from, and where we are going (as Darwin and Freud tried to do), it is inescapably mythic.

Literature and mathematics are related because they both take their root ideas from myth, but because literature performs the root idea in a personified way, in which the planets, seas, and rivers are experienced as spirits, it is a democratization of myth. Mathematics is a mystery school for initiates, but literature is open even to children. If we look back over the four cultural ecologies, we can see that for each of these epochs, a particular literary masterpiece sums up the adaptation of consciousness to the ecology of a time and space.

As an adaptation to an ecology, literature behaves ecologically in more ways than one. Like a forest moving through the stages of succession to climax, literature unfolds through three stages of succession: (1) formative, (2) dominant, and (3) climactic. The formative work enters into a new ecological niche of consciousness, the dominant work stabilizes the mentality, and the climactic work finishes it.

The formative work for the Riverine cultural ecology is the Sumerian cycle of poems on the courtship of Inanna and Dumuzi.[20] In this love cycle one can still see the historical horizon of the transition from agricultural village to town, for many of the poems are really work songs that maidens could sing teasingly to men as they would beat the churn up and down to make butter.[21] Other poems are competitions between the shepherd and the farmer for the goddess's favors, but all of the poems are clear celebrations of the new agricultural ways of life that are formative of civilization.

The dominant work of the Riverine is the Akkadian poem

"Inanna's Descent into the Nether World," a poem in which civilization is now expressed, not in work songs for the churning of butter or celebrations of the shepherd over the farmer, but in priestcraft. The "Descent" is no villager's poem, but a highly complex investigation into the cosmological dimensions of the planetary balances between order and chaos, civilization and savagery, earth and the heavens.

The climactic work for the Riverine cultural ecology is the great *Gilgamesh Epic*. Climactic works, like formative ones, are Janus-headed and face in two directions: they sum up and finish a world view and also point prophetically to a world to come. In its meditation on death and the slaying of the spirit of the forest, the *Gilgamesh Epic* was prophetic in its study of deforestation, the civilized alienation of the ego, and the limits of masculine military power; and all of these themes were to become characteristic of the tragic history of human experience in the succeeding Mediterranean epoch.

The formative works of the Mediterranean cultural ecology are the Homeric epics. The *Odyssey* quite directly sets up the horizons of the Mediterranean landscape in the voyages of Odysseus, but the epic also establishes the basic theme of the alienation of human consciousness from its source, and the yawning gulf that separates male from female, location from home. The epic forms an archetypal pattern that is to dominate literature for millennia, for contemporary works as different as James Joyce's *Ulysses* and Nicholas Roeg's *The Man Who Fell to Earth* are but modern material cut from the ancient pattern.

The *Iliad,* which seems to me much older and more

archaic in tone than the *Odyssey,* is the primary work that establishes the world view of order and entropy, consciousness and violence, history and vanishing. So formative is this particular work that I feel that the roots of philosophy and science are here in this *whole* work and not in the more recognized fragments of the Pre-Socratics.

The dominant masterpiece of the Mediterranean is the *Oresteia,* for it expresses what is to be the enduring structure of Western culture: the displacement of relationship by abstraction. Instructed by a male god of light, Apollo, the son kills the mother, displaces the rule of ancient matrilineal custom, and moves out of the tribe into the polis in a celebration of patriarchy, law, and rationality. For the geometrizing mentality of the Greeks, the entire world becomes reorganized, not in the kinship systems enumerated by Hesiod, but in the new mentality of abstraction in which the chorus distances itself from the *skene* at the same time that culture separates itself from nature in the polis.

The climactic work of the Mediterranean, one that completely finishes the mentality in the way that only a great genius can, is Dante's *Divine Comedy.* The ancient Mediterranean goddess, who had been displaced from the earth, is now set up in the heavens, and Orestes's polis is transformed into Dante's ecclesia. Reason, which had slain the mother of nature through abstraction, is now wed to consciousness through "the love that moves the sun and other stars." The geometrizing mentality, which had initiated a process of distancing from nature, now finds its true ideal realm in heaven. *Ratio* becomes sublimated into *intellectus,* and the souls of alienated humanity gather in the petals of the White Rose. Pattern flowers.

The formative work for the Atlantic cultural ecology, one that shows the shift from medievalism to modernism, is Cervantes's *Don Quixote,* a work that for quite different reasons both McLuhan and Foucault chose as the exemplar of cultural transformation. Inspired by a fantastic literature, the equivalent of the communications media of our day, the solitary knight of the sad countenance rides forth in pursuit of a lost culture. Precisely when the traditional culture is about to break up, when the universal ecclesia is about to be replaced by a universal economy, and when the aristocrat on his horse is about to be replaced by the capitalist, the last knight rides forth. But Don Quixote is not so much a man of the past as of the future. The individual alone with his fantasies, fantasies that alter his very perception of reality, is not a man of the medieval or the classical world. He is the first modern man whose world view has been transformed, not by parents or priests, but by the media. Precisely because modernism is a wrenching away of the solitary individual from the traditional community, madness becomes the concern of the new age of the mind. Whether we are gazing at the paintings of Bosch, or hearing the cry of Lear on the heath, or watching Don Quixote wear a barber's bowl and call it Mambrino's helmet, we are trying to come to terms with the manner in which the mind creates reality for itself.

The rise of the individual with the new definitions of selfhood is quintessentially a modern phenomenon, and such a cultural appearance is marked by the appearance of new literary genres, such as autobiography. At the formative stage of emergence from tradition, the solitary individual might feel the pull of madness as the way in which the individual could create a personal cultural envelopment, but as the mind begins to grow confident of itself and begins with Leibniz to celebrate reason as sufficient to understand and control nature, being, very capitalistically, begins to sell its soul for knowing. Knowing begins to eliminate being, creating the tragic irony that knowing really doesn't know, and in the attempt to control nature, the mind simply becomes the captive of instinctive appetites. The dominant work, therefore, of the Atlantic cultural ecology is *Faust*.

But by *Faust* I do not simply mean the work of Goethe. Lévi-Strauss has argued that every variation of a myth is a performance of the myth and that even Freud's theory of the Oedipus complex is a performance of the myth of Oedipus.[22] In much the same way, the works of Marlowe, Goethe, Spengler, Gounod, and Thomas Mann are all chapters of the larger European work that is *Faust*. Before the West had such creatures as scientists manipulating the genetic code, Renaissance man imagined the alchemist who sold his soul to the devil, and intuited the shape of things to come. In many ways Marlowe's Faust seems to speak to our contemporary situation even more than Goethe's romantic Faust, for Marlowe's man becomes caught up in the banality of power, of fetching tropical fruits in winter or satisfying his lust for control; but the very satisfaction of the desire to control only leads to enslavement. Knowing can never become being; so only the spirit can unmask the covering over with which the mind bewitched itself.

The climactic work of the Atlantic epoch is *Finnegans*

Wake. Coming from a marginal culture at the very edge of Europe, James Joyce very consciously finished Europe. First, he finished the remains of the Mediterranean vision in his *Ulysses,* a work that ends in the affirmation of the feminine brought down out of Dante's heaven and put to bed. Then, having finished with the voyages of the solitary individual afloat on a stream of consciousness, Joyce went on to express the transition from print-isolated humanity in its book-lined study to H.C.E., Here Comes Everybody. At the time when the hardy objects of a once materialistic science disappear into subatomic particles, so characters as egos with discrete identities disappear to become patterns of *corso-ricorso,* and history becomes the performance of myth. Characterization is replaced by allusion, and as pattern and configuration become more important than persons, Joyce brings us to the end of the age of individualism. But like Moses on Mount Pisgah gazing into a Promised Land he cannot enter, Joyce brings us to the end of modernism, but he himself cannot pass over into the hieroglyphic thought of the Pacific-Aerospace cultural ecology to come.

McLuhan considered *Finnegans Wake* to be the prophetic work that pointed to the arrival of electronic, post-civilized humanity, the creature of changing roles who lives "mythically and in depth." Obviously, we are now only in the early days of the transition from the Atlantic cultural ecology of the European epoch to the Pacific-Space cultural ecology of the planetary epoch, and so no one knows for certain just where these electronic and aerospace technologies are taking us. But since I grew up in Los Angeles, and not in Dublin or Paris, I have a few hunches.

The emergence of the new Pacific-Space cultural ecology is related to the historical events of World War II for several reasons. Hiroshima announced the beginnings of the atomic age, and the airplane industries of the West Coast were to be rather quickly transformed into aerospace technologies. With the postwar rise to greatness of Stanford and Berkeley, and with the emergence of Silicon Valley, the Pacific Shift of America from Europe to Japan was irresistible.

Perhaps in the next generation or two, a great artist from one of the cultures on the Pacific Rim will create the formative work of art for this new culture, to do for the Pacific what Homer did long ago for the Mediterranean world. This imagined masterpiece may not be literary, for it is hard to deny that the rise of film, television, and computer graphics has created a new sensibility that cannot be expressed in exclusively literary form. The Homeric epics were popular art forms, ones meant to be recited at social gatherings, and so we should not fear that new popular art forms mean the death of literary culture. When oral culture encountered writing, literature was created. If literature encounters video cassettes that have computer animation wed to music, literature will simply reincarnate into a new form; it will not die.

As catastrophe theory continues to evolve into multidimensional morphologies, and as film, television, and computer graphics become democratized through personal computers and VCRs, the right hemisphere of the brain will be stimulated by a new form of visual thinking that I prefer to call the return of hieroglyphic thinking, because this designation suggests a new synthesis of art, science, and religion. I may be wrong about the emergence of a new mentality, for there is much in genetic engineering and capitalistic ecology that can force nature and culture into mechanistic forms of control. The future may be an earth that is a space colony *on* earth: a canned civilization of total control and rational management. But if the larger ecology of Mind is always beyond the limits of the controls of conscious purpose, and if wildness and catastrophes are nature's protection against the forms of rationalization that would make an ecology a closed system, then I trust that nature has her Gaian resources to defend herself. If acid rain, the Greenhouse Effect, or other disasters from dioxin or genetic engineering continue to alter the environment drastically, then I believe that the new mentality will finds its *kairos*, its appropriate season of action.

Until such a time of political change or the emergence of an artistic masterpiece that is formative of the new culture, I must make use of what is ready-to-hand. One experimental work that that expressed both a Pacific-Aerospace orientation and visual, mythological thinking was Disney's *Fantasia*, especially his rendering of Stravinsky's *Rite of Spring*.

All scholarship is disguised autobiography; so I am, no doubt, going back to the fact that I saw *Fantasia* before I knew how to read. For a five-year-old child in 1943, the experience of sitting in a dark cave and watching a vision of the evolution of the earth was a religious experience. No *rite de passage* for an initiate at Lascaux or Eleusis could have been more transporting than that wedding of Bach, Tchaikovsky, and Stravinsky to images of the larger universe.

Before I had known only a neighborhood in a large city, but when I came out of that cave, I knew that I was part of something much bigger, an entire universe.

It is probably for such reasons that I have no Luddite's fear of technology, but feel instead that the new developments in computer animation are the beginnings of a new mentality. I look forward to a time when instead of sitting in front of an electronic typewriter to create, for example, the second chapter of this book, I will be able to sit at a console and compose a video cassette that will have the complex crystals of color, the voice-overs, and the music I choose to accompany them. And then I hope to be able to slip the cassette into a modem on my phone and send it to all the subscribers in the satellite network who care for this kind of thing. We are being told that the age of mass audiences is over and that because there are not that many people out there who care for things as esoteric as ideas, "narrow-casting" is replacing broadcasting; so it seems a waste of trees to try to guess how many people will want to buy the book. Better to have subscribers than customers when it comes to philosophy and *Wissenskunst.*

And yet, old capitalistic Disney is there to prove that new art forms need not be elitist. What could be more populist than Disneyland?

In an early study of industrial society entitled *Hard Times,* Dickens contrasted the world of the factory with the world of the circus. The factory was the place of *Homo faber,* but the circus was the place of *Homo ludens,* the place where misfits fit, where the body was revealed, where

human beings sported with their ancient companions, the
beasts; it was the place where feelings and affection could
triumph over utilitarian rationality. What Dickens pro-
jected as the mirror opposite of Victorian Manchester has,
in fact, now become California. The circus may have faded,
but its role as a community of play has been taken over by
Disneyland and Disney World. And just as the circus was
an affront to Victorian seriousness, so the kitsch of Disneyland is an affront to modern sophistication. And yet, there
seems to be something occult about these cartoon characters, something almost religious that is at a deeper level of
consciousness than intellectual sophistication. The ani-
mated figures (recall the Latin root for animation) seem to
be parodies of archetypes that still appeal to the archetypes
of the collective unconscious. In spite of the kitsch, the
vulgar sentimentalizations of the past, from animal totem-
ism to Greek paganism, the unconscious is called forth.
Could it be that the community of the future is not a polis
in which abstraction triumphs, but a city of *Homo ludens*
in which incarnation itself is recognized to be the ego as
video game of the *Daimon?* Perhaps the elitist *Finnegans
Wake,* or Ezra Pound's *Cantos* for that matter, are not that
far apart in structure from populist Disneyland, for in all
three artifacts many histories and cultures are simultaneously exposed in a single space.

There is, of course, a shadow side to this Pacific world,
and Ronald Reagan is definitely the shadow of Walt Disney.
Reagan is the man of no identity but only roles, the man
who confuses both Europe and the East Coast by approach-

ing the presidency not as a task but as a performance. Small wonder that President Mitterand of France, the literary intellectual, found nothing he could relate to in the void of character that is the personality of Reagan.

If Ronald Reagan is the shadow of Walt Disney, it teaches us not to slip into a futurism in which we imagine that there will be no evil in our hoped-for new culture. There was evil and a dark shadow to the Riverine, Mediterranean, and Atlantic cultural ecologies, and I suspect that there will be a planetary shadow to a planetary culture.

The problem of evil, as it is affectionately known in the trade, is a considerable obstruction in the path of futurism, utopianism, or even the larger descriptions of cultural ecology, for if ideologies are expressions of a false consciousness that prevent people from knowing what they are doing, how can choice, of good or of evil, enter into the patterning of behavior, individual or collective?

If there can be distinct narrative forms to the modes of mathematical articulation for an epoch, as well as for the archetypal literary masterpieces that sum up an era, then there should also be rather pronounced shifts in the descriptions of religious experience, in the cultural forms of encountering good and evil, as Western civilization moves from one cultural ecology into another.

Deciding what to look for in science or history is, of course, the first step in finding it; consequently, it did not take me long to imagine the following pattern:

Religious Mode of Experience	Archetypal Religious Leader
I. Momentary possession	I. Dumuzi
II. Surrender to authority	II. Moses
III. Commitment to belief	III. Luther
IV. Symbiotic consciousness	IV. The group as an ecology of consciousness

Characteristic Good	Characteristic Evil
I. Humble piety	I. Pride, arrogant assertion of self
II. Obedience to law	II. Revolt against authority
III. Understanding doctrine	III. Ecstatic escape or transcendence
IV. Universal compassion	IV. Collectivization through terror

Re-ligare means "to bind"; therefore, the religious experience is one that binds part to whole, individual to culture, culture to nature. Because knowing is a "fall" from Being in the sense, as Bateson put it, that consciousness only reports on the products of our perceptions, knowing cannot report on the neurophysiological processes with which those products of knowledge are set up. Consciousness, then, will be in its structure an inherently limited horizon. The religious impulse will, therefore, be one that tries to reunite knowing with Being. Since consciousness finds itself in a time frame of the present, the first religious compulsion is to reunite the present with either a prophetically imagined future or, more often, a past antecedent to the "fall" into consciousness. Earlier cultures become the metaphor for preconsciousness, and part of the atavistic power of religion comes from its ability to evoke memories of earlier states in the cultural evolution of Mind. In the world of the city, it calls out with the imagery of the farmer; in the world of the farm, it calls out with the imagery of the shepherd; in the world of the herdsman, it calls out with the imagery of the cave and the ancient hunt, or with the imagery of the Great Mother who reigned for the millennia before the herdsman discovered paternity and property in keeping watch over his flocks.

Religious experience is in many ways incredibly reactionary; it does not suffer well the given conditions of any present. In the world of civilized and conscious man, it evokes the ancient collective mind when consciousness was bound, not by a wall, but by a permeable membrane. And so for civilized man the basic religious experience is to be drawn back in trance, in momentary possession by the ancient goddess or animal spirit.

Julian Jaynes sees the origin of consciousness in the sixth century b.c. and claims that before that time the twin hemispheres of the brain were not in communication with one another through the bridge of the corpus callosum, and so experiences of the right hemisphere were perceived to be outside the body in voice or vision.[23] This description is fascinating, for it is a scientific form of paranoia, a form of misplaced concreteness that yet in its paranoia intuits something that is going on and that has been missed by normal observers. Scientific fundamentalism, like religious fundamentalism, is always too simple, and Jaynes's attempt to map locations in the brain with states of consciousness needs

to be corrected with the more sophisticated neurophysiology of Humberto Maturana and Francisco Varela [24]; but
Jaynes's perceptions can be seen as a recognition of the
emergence of the hard and discrete ego.

There is a feedback of civilization onto individuation, and
so it is that Bronze Age changes in burial patterns do spell
out changes in the ways of life and not just in the ways of
death. In megalithic culture the bones are placed inside the
tumulus in great anonymous heaps. But in the shift from
matrilineal to patrilineal, there is a shift in emphasis to
warfare and the military hero who wins himself a personal
tomb, and a shift to the accumulation of private property in
life that is held by sons who can keep watch over the tombs
as the markers of their own dynastic legitimacy.

The ancient Neolithic metaphysic of the male as metaphor of vanishing, as metaphor of the instantaneous temporal modality, is still maintained; but now, in the historical
turn of the spiral, the temporality is not associated with just
any male who plays the role of the dying god of the dying
year; it is associated with a particular male with a particular
historical career of conquest. For tribal man, life is a cycle
of Nietzsche's Eternal Return; the self is not hard and
discrete, and one lives with one's dead, with the animals,
with the spirits of place, and with the gods of the sky. Death
is no great tragedy, and the funeral (as it still is in Ireland)
is one of the dominant celebrations of life.

But with the shift from matrilineal to patrilineal, the
cycle of the Great Mother is exchanged for the dynastic
lines of the Great Father. Private property is won by war and
passed on to sons. Religious experience, in this historical

context, is to be called back by the goddess to the prehistorical world of the feminine. The linked opposite to accumulation is loss, and so the great problem for male culture, one that is explored in the *Gilgamesh Epic,* is the problem of death. A name is the definition of the ego, but as Gilgamesh and Enkidu go out to make a name for themselves, they discover death. In slaying the spirit of the forest, in cutting down the world of cycles and Eternal Return, they anger the goddess, and she sees to it that Gilgamesh's beloved companion is put to death: not to a male heroic death in battle, but a natural death, that is to say a feminine death, of rotting away in disease and in bed. But the goddess is not able to bring down the whole masculine world, and so Gilgamesh the king survives, and with him his city and its civilization. The poem ends as it began, with a poetic meditation on the hard wall that divides culture from nature.

The hard wall around the city is also the hard armor around the newly emerged self, but this self is a fragile creature that can easily be taken back. Ancient woman as the goddess can easily return from her journey in the underworld beneath civilization to assert her dominance over the processes of life and death. Man will remain the metaphor of vanishing, and dynasties will come and go, but Lilith will always be there to dance in the ruins of male vanities.

Different cultures will find different forms of expression to deal with this metaphysic of male vanishing and female continuity, but whether the man as priest puts on woman's dress, or cuts off his genitals to put them on the altar of the Great Mother, or subincises his penis to make it look like a vulva, or has his head cut off by a gang of women who fling it back, still singing, on the collective sea, the structural condition of the cultural arrangement is still the same: the ego is being annihilated and pulled back atavistically into the collective.

And so for civilized man, the mode of religious experience is momentary possession: momentary possession in sexual intercourse with the goddess (*hieros gamos,* sacred marriage) or momentary possession in a trance communication with the god *(genius loci).*

The Sumerian figure of Dumuzi expresses a cultural pattern that is still close to the Neolithic. Dumuzi as the shepherd-king is raised on high by the goddess Inanna and then torn to shreds by her demons when he becomes proud and forgetful of the feminine power that put him on the throne. Dumuzi as the male is still dependent on the female; he is not a military hero who sets up a dynasty to hold onto male power through sons.

When the civilizational process has consolidated its hold on human culture, then the mode of religious experience begins to shift. No longer is one simply drawn back into shamanistic possession by animal spirit or god; now religious experience becomes articulated by a priesthood. Consequently, religious experience begins to be seen as surrender to authority, as obedience to law. Whether the figure of authority is Pharoah or Moses, the pattern is the same: religious value is expressed in obedience to law.

The archetypal figure of this level is indeed Moses, the man with the great historic destiny, the man with the enormous identity. Dumuzi, though proud and forgetful of Inanna, is not greatly individuated. He is still very close to the Neolithic anonymity of the vanishing male god; he is only something because of Inanna. But Moses is so great and so completely individuated that his enormity prevents him from entering the Promised Land. It is only the truly obedient, routine-operational manager Joshua who is allowed to take the people into the land of Israel.

In comparing Hebrew and Sumerian mythologies, we can begin to appreciate the difference between a *formative* culture and a *pivotal* one within a cultural ecology. The Sumerians and the Greeks are formative cultures, the one of Riverine and the other of Mediterranean. The Hebrews are the pivotal culture in the shift from Riverine into Mediterranean. Pivotal cultures are reactionary in a positive sense, for they articulate the past in a way that allows it to be digested and transcended. The Greeks are the formative force for what will become natural history, mathematics, and science; the Hebrews are the reactionary force for what will become the Abrahamic religions.

The importance of reactionary, pivotal cultures can be seen today in the case of the Japanese. The Californians are the formative force of the Pacific, but the Japanese are the traditional and reactionary force. Therefore, one should expect that Japanese-Californian Zen Buddhism will continue to play a great role in the future. Christianity is reform Judaism; so the future will probably see some version of reform Buddhism emerging in the Pacific Rim that will become the counterbalance to the new technologies, much in the same way that the Abrahamic religions served as the conservative counterbalance to Western science.

The importance of reactionary, pivotal cultures is also seen in the case of the English, for in spite of their eighteenth-century Industrial Revolution, they did not create either the Atlantic or the Pacific-Aerospace cultural ecologies. The Spanish and the Dutch were more formative of the Atlantic, and the Americans of the Pacific; but in their global empire, the British were the great monarchical, reactionary force that struggled to consolidate the world into a vision of moral order.

Formative cultures express the creative expansion into new space, whereas pivotal cultures express the consolidation into tradition. The Hebrews are, therefore, concerned with surrender to authority in the obedience to law, but the development of Greek philosophy is to challenge authority and to replace obedience with understanding. For these reasons, I see our conventional designation of Greeks and Hebrews as ancestral to be correct; but their roles in shaping us are different.

In the social development of religion, priesthood soon becomes priestcraft, and temples degenerate in the Weberian "routinization of charisma" that turns revelation into bureaucracy. But as old religious forms begin to become overripe and rotten, new forms of religious experience begin to emerge in the new civilizational context of intense individuation. Newly equipped with personal identities, individuals are not so ready to submit simply to obedience to law, and so the mental understanding of doctrine becomes more critical than simply identifying with a cultural definition of the group through a religion. The covenant of Jeremiah is not handed down on tablets; it is written in the individual's heart.

The individual prophet is chosen by God, not by the institutions of humans. For a while, Samuel tried to interpret his chosenness as the divine foundation of a spiritual dynasty, but as his sons fell and began having intercourse with Canaanite temple prostitutes, it became clear that sons could not hold spiritual power as sons had held political power. In the brilliance of the ecology of Mind expressed in the Old Testament, innovation becomes protected as prophecy is randomized. Man cannot know which one among him will be chosen by God to become a prophet.

The Old Testament is a pivotal document in the cultural evolution of consciousness in a score of ways. The Near Eastern monarch was a symbol of the body politic and a cultural definition of identity, but the prophetic leaders of the Old Testament discovered that history is a medium through which the mind moves to its destiny with God. It can be said, then, that the discovery of history is part of an interior process of gaining identity through prophetic recognition of one's relation to the culture, the historical movement, and the messianic destiny that waits at the end of history. In effect, the radical innovation of prophecy, in its challenge of institutional priesthoods, is a revolutionary discovery of individuality. Suddenly kingship, wealth, and tribal lineage are put to the side in a psychological definition of value that affirms the power of the individual to embody the presence of God.

Civilizations have parents, and for this being we call the West, Greece is the father and Israel is the mother. When Christianity, as reform Judaism, weds the natural philosophy of the Greeks to the discovery of history by the Hebrew prophets, European civilization is the issue. The pattern is repeated in the Reformation, for when capitalism is wed to Protestantism, industrial civilization is the issue. And now that reform Buddhism is being wed to cybernetics, the Pacific Basin is pregnant with a whole new civilization.

Precisely because prophecy is an emphasis on the value of the individual, the individual becomes the space in which the cultural drama takes place. With this emphasis on the growth of the individual mind, the understanding of doctrine becomes critical. The new *agon* becomes one of prophet against priest, and whether it is a case of Elijah against the prophets of Baal, or Luther against the Pope, the paradigm is the same. When a culture has advanced to the point where private property is mental, then understanding of doctrine challenges the old cultural pattern of Mosaic obedience to law.

For the greater part of the world at this moment, this is as far as humanity has spiritually progressed, and the religious warfare in India, the Middle East, and Northern Ireland is the old battle of obedience to law versus understanding of doctrine. And if the paramilitary cults of the extreme Right in the United States had their way, this religious warfare would be brought home with a vengeance. This old cultural paradigm does not want to die from a peaceful old age, but is bent on putting all the infidels to the sword, and since religion, by its very nature, has a strong atavistic power to pull people back into the ecstatic seizures of the previous level of consciousness, we are not likely to make it into a new Pacific-Aerospace cultural ecology without the religious wars that characterized the beginnings of the Atlantic cultural ecology.

But since negation is a form of emphasis, the era of religious intolerance, hysteria, and violence will also serve to turn people away from religion in disgust. Religious warfare is now, and will be most likely in the future, one of the cultural forces that pushes people out of religion into a new kind of scientific spirituality (an ethos already expressed by such people as Whitehead and Einstein) that will be to Protestant fundamentalism what Quakerism is to Roman Catholicism. As the mind of religion takes us into cultural entropy by breaking up into smaller and smaller sects, and as the old pattern of the understanding of doctrine degenerates into the violence of schism against schism (and one can already see this happening in modern Israel), then perhaps some future prophetic ecologist will arise to say, "The sun is One, but many and different are the flowers it brightens." At that point of religious exhaustion, humanity will pass from the stage of the mental definitions of doctrine, from ideology, to an ecology of consciousness experienced through a universal compassion for all sentient beings. The age of religious conversion will be over, and one will accept a sacred tradition as one accepts a favored poet or composer in an artistic tradition: according to one's inner needs at the moment. Spirituality, like artistic or scientific ability, cannot be dynastic, and parents will begin to realize that they cannot pass on their Catholicism, Judaism, or fundamentalism to their children.

As Luther is the archetypal figure of modernism, with his heroic individuality, I imagine that the archetypal figure for the cultural level of universal compassion will be the group, the *sangha*, or the mystical body of Christ. I see popular art forms such as Philip Glass's score for *Koyaanisqatsi* or Paul Winter's jazz mass *Missa Gaia* as performances of this archetype. Architecturally, the Lindisfarne Chapel in the Sangre de Cristo Mountains of southern Colorado is another invocation of this shift in cultural levels from religion to spirituality.

The most important civilizational force in this cultural evolution from religion to spirituality is Western science. The general public fears that science is a threat to religion and the liberal arts because there are always a few simplistic fundamentalists of scientism, people like B. F. Skinner, Marvin Minsky, and E. O. Wilson, who catch reporters' attention by proclaiming that the mind doesn't exist, or that creativity is a fake and that the brain is a computer made out of meat, or that the state can be replaced by sociobiological management. These statements make citizens feel that their days are numbered and that they are about to become subjects, first of research, then of controls. There is much to fear in the social institution of science, for the sick in the United States tend to lose their civil liberties; indeed, this kind of science is what the Inquisition was to Catholicism: a hideous degeneration of a bureaucracy given too much power. If the state does not intervene to give power to mediocrity, science has certain built-in self-correcting mechanisms that keep it healthy, for science is basically a spiritual enterprise. Science is reform Christianity; it is to Christianity what Christianity is to Judaism, or what Buddhism is to Hinduism: a visionary simplification. Science is totally dependent on a love of the truth and a spirit of fellowship, and if lust for power and careerist ambitions bring about a situation in which scientists start lying to one another, the whole culture falls apart immediately. In religion, priests can lie to one another about whether salvation requires total immersion or only sprinkling; but if scientists start lying about the results of their research, the institution goes into shock, and very powerful forces of self-correction are brought into play.

Science can become evil, but so can religion, art, and politics, for anything human can become evil. But what we can see from the cultural movements from one historical level to another is that evil plays a role in the process of manifestation. For each cultural ecology there is a characteristic good and, by linked opposition, a characteristic evil. If humble piety is the good that enables one to submit to momentary possession by the goddess or the god in *hieros gamos,* or trance, then pride and an arrogant assertion of the self is the evil act that blocks the good. When Dumuzi becomes arrogant to sit on the throne while Inanna goes through hell, he displays the classic pride that goeth before a fall.

All of which is familiar enough, but what is not familiar is the fact that this evil is the signal of emergence to the next level of historical order. Pride and self-assertion are needed to move from momentary possession to the stable identity capable of making a commitment to obedience to law. It would seem that there is an isomorphic relation between evil and environmental pollution, and that in both cases a form

of noise or dissonance is a signal of emergence from one level
of order to another. Similarly, when priesthoods have stabil-
ized religion in the form of obedience to law, then evil
becomes revolt against authority. But this kind of revolt
points up the mental development of a new relativism, for
clearly Moses's revolt against Pharoah is evil in Egypt but
good in Israel. And in much the same way, Luther's revolt
against the Papacy is seen as good by Protestants and evil
by Catholics. So the evil of revolt against authority is actually the signal of the shift to the next level, commitment to
belief, with its characteristic good of the understanding of
doctrine.

For the Atlantic cultural ecology, the good is seen as the
understanding of doctrine, and if you are a follower of the
Pope, Jerry Falwell, or the Ayatollah Khomeini, that is as far
as you wish to go.

If the good is expressed in the "true" doctrine, then the
evil is ecstatic escape or transcendence of moralistic definitions. For fundamentalists the rock music, drugs, and cults
of the young are clearly the work of the Devil. From an
ecological point of view, the cults and the counterculture are
like weeds in a monocrop field: they are responses to the
artificial devastations of industrialization and temporary
efforts to rescue the soil as the field moves through succession back to the natural diversity of tall-grass prairie or
climax forest.

Good at one level of order becomes evil at another, and
evil at one level of order becomes good at another. In the
age of mental understanding of doctrine, obedience to law
is evil, for it aborts the development of the mind. In an age

of universal compassion, understanding of doctrine becomes evil, for it simply sanctifies murder in religious warfare. But universal compassion is shadowed by what Erich Kahler called "collectivization through terror,"[25] a psychological technique in which the frightened and alienated individual is comforted by terror and gathered back into an ideology in which the ego is annihilated by the collective.

Terror destroys integrity, the wholeness of autonomous unities; but terror is often used to describe mystical or erotic transfiguration. As Rilke has put it in the *Duino Elegies,* "*Denn das Schöne ist nichts / als des Schrecklichen An-fang . . .*" (But Beauty is nothing but / The beginning of Terror . . .).

Terror is a crushing integration, the *eros* of rape rather than love. The difficulty arises when we stop to consider that many religious practices are isomorphic to evil acts, for both can work by the logic of inversion. If the normal man eats, the monk fasts; if the normal man accumulates, the monk lives in poverty; if the normal woman makes love and has children, the nun lives in celibacy. For both sanctity and evil, reversal is the pattern. How, then, can one tell the difference?

If evil can be the signal of emergence from one level of religious experience to another, and if pollution can be the signal of the emergence of a new level of historical order, then what, in Bateson's words, is "the difference that makes a difference"? How do we know when it is appropriate to practice an evil action to approach a higher good, as when Moses rejects Pharoah or Luther rejects the Pope? And how do we recognize that an evil act is simply horrible, as when

the Israeli terrorists tried to murder all the Arab mayors of
the West Bank, or when the Ayatollah tried to eliminate all
the Bahais in Iran by firing squad?

All the most moving and important performances of
knowing in our lives are unknowable. How do we know that
we love someone? What is the process of recognition by
which we determine that we are in love with one person and
not another? It seems as if it were analagous to aesthetic
knowledge, a similar process of recognition in which we are
re-membered in great music. But what is this knowledge of
discrimination that tells us that Bach is greater than heavy
metal; that the Cathedral of Chartres is the living body
of an angel, but that Notre Dame is a tourists' museum;
that Rockefeller Plaza is a public space, but that the
Trump Tower is a vulgar piece of Los Angeles stuck into
Manhattan?

Aesthetic knowledge is a feeling about knowing; it is a
commentary on the processes of perception themselves.
Through the functioning of this metalevel of discrimination
we can recognize that we can be mistaken in our knowing,
and even, if we have the kind of aesthetic discrimination
called wisdom, wrong in our religious experiences, mistaking
some psychic experience, vision, or para-noia, for knowledge, when it is only an interpretation of intimations. Because all these mysterious moments of knowing, in love or
art, are unknowable, the unknowing kind of knowledge
brings us closer to Being. Normal knowing and opinions
cannot map Being any more than a bucket can sound the
sea; but aesthetic knowing is the art of swimming, the grace-
ful presence that realizes you do not have to measure the sea
to love it, sail on it, or swim in it.

When knowing becomes conscious of its limitations and then turns on them to make the limited process into a dance that talks about the relationship between knowing and the unknowable, it performs Being. This is what both Bateson and Heidegger were trying to get at in affirming thinking: thinking Being. It is difficult to think Being in philosophy, and for me Heidegger's *Being and Time* is a monumental failure; but sometimes we learn more in life from failures than from success.

Thinking Being is difficult in philosophy, but it is easier in music, art, and architecture, and, perhaps, in *Wissenskunst.* The map is not the territory, but some maps do help us to find our way home; and yet, home is precisely the place where we no longer need maps.

Humanity is not yet at home in this world of earth; so presumably we still have need of philosophy. And what Bateson's philosophy can teach us about our battles between good and evil is that "the difference that makes a difference" is difference itself. Evil is the destruction of differences; good is the creation of ever new differences. Differences are vital, and the good emphasizes diversity, individuation, integrity, and participation in the universal through the unique. Evil is just who Goethe's Mephistopheles said he was: "The spirit I, that endlessly denies, / And rightly, too; for all that comes to birth / Is fit for overthrow, as nothing worth."

Evil works through collectivization, not individuation, with the unit crushed into the uniform, the mind crushed into a cult. This is the difference that makes a difference between isomorphic groups: between the followers of Rudolph Steiner and Adolph Hitler, between the communities of Findhorn and Rajneeshpuram, between a tall-grass prairie and the animal concentration camp of a feed lot in Kansas.

Because the good works through the unique and not the uniform, it is not possible to standardize it through time. Each moment and historical situation is unique, and so the good repeated in an inappropriate situation can become evil. It takes a mind to know a difference, and so no catechism or moral standardization can dispense with the need for a mind to know when a situation is good and when it is evil. Abstract justice in one context can become cruelty; liberal kindness in another context can create evil and enormous suffering. The knowledge of the appropriate season of action, the *kairos* (which is surely an ecological metaphor if there ever was one), is universal compassion: universal because it is extended to the entire ecology of all sentient beings, and compassionate because such right mindfulness is tough-minded and not sentimental.

People who lack compassion often have a secret fear of evil within themselves that they try to mask by loudly screaming and pointing the finger at someone else as being the instrument of evil. I have had some experience with people of this mentality who are members of paramilitary right-wing extremist groups in the American West, so I recognize the orientation when it comes out in a political personality such as the Ayatollah Khomeini. People who scream about others being possessed by the Devil are generally possessed themselves, and their lack of compassion comes about because they cannot confront the evil inside themselves and are trying to murder it outside by becoming a murderer. Jung was certainly right in his analysis of the shadow, for those who can own their own projections, and can see their own shadows, are certainly the ones who can be more secure and forgiving of others. Humans are very social and plastic creatures, and when put into a certain context, they can be capable of any evil. Only when we have compassion for ourselves, by recognizing the capacity for evil within ourselves as well as in the historical process of manifestation, can we begin to move from ideological hysteria to the ecology of consciousness that the Christians call *agapé* and the Buddhists call compassion.

This knowledge of the ontological role of evil has been with us esoterically for some time, but it is difficult for an ordinary ego to deal with it. The ordinary soul wants a simple list of *Don't's;* it does not want a vision of complexity. However, the knowledge is there in the New Testament, for Judas cannot go out to betray Jesus until Jesus empowers him to do so. Jesus performs a shadow eucharist by giving Judas a sop of bread in vinegar, and only then can the spirit of evil take him over so that he can betray Jesus to bring about the redemption that requires crucifixion. Milton only half-consciously recognized this difficult understanding, for in *Paradise Lost* he makes Lucifer and Christ associated as the two sides of an unrecognized demiurge. When Lucifer is thinking "one step higher makes me highest," that is when God the Father announces the emanation of the Son. As Milton explores the nature of evil, it is no accident that Satan is the tragic hero of the epic and that God the Father is a boring psychopomp. One can feel no compassion for God, but the increasing degeneration of Satan is tragic.

If Lucifer and Christ are twin forces of manifestation, the

two sides of the demiurge of creation, then we cannot kill evil without ourselves becoming evil killers. Our only way out of this logical dilemma is to love our enemy, which, of course, is exactly what Jesus told us to do. The fundamentalist, whether Christian or Islamic, sees devils everywhere and becomes what he or she hates.

The problem that Milton faced in dealing with evil is one we all face, for we simply cannot function as an ordinary human being endowed with an ego if we accept evil as part of a cosmic process. We cannot simply look at Buchenwald and say, "This is good, for Israel will come out of this." Such a response would be equivocation and not compassion.

It would seem that, like a flashlight searching for darkness and dispelling it in the act of looking for it, human beings cannot operate with an ego and come to terms with evil. Our only way of accepting its ontology is to violently reject it. Our excretions are intimate and personal and tell much about what we chose to take in as food, but the only proper ecological response to excrement is to keep it away from ourselves. But, to continue the metaphor, if we push it too far away, it accumulates and becomes a greater problem; if we remain conscious of its presence and recycle it, it becomes fertilizer.

So, it would seem, that when we repress evil violently, we become violent repressors of others; but if evil is known and put in its proper distance from us, new life springs up as we gain compassion.

Today the overwhelming evil is collectivization through terror in all its forms, from political torture to warfare, from thermonuclear terrorizing of the whole world by the military collusion of the "U.S.S.S.R.," to a poisoning of the biosphere that is bringing the whole human race into one deadly toxic dump called civilization. What is this evil telling us?

If evil announces the next level of historical order, then evil is expressing the coming planetary culture. Unconsciously, the world is one, for global pollution spells out a dark integration that does not honor the rational boundaries of the nation-states. And so, industrial nation-states in their fullest development have contributed to their own end. Collectivization, then, must mean that the future is some sort of collective consciousness in which the completely individuated and conscious ego becomes surrounded by the permeable membrane of an ecology of Mind and not by the wall of civilization.

Rock festivals in particular, and rock music in general, seem to express this fascination with collectivization. Since we have become an electronic society, a society of information, it is not surprising that the pollution of the new cultural ecology is noise and paranoia. Rock music is about the relationship between information and noise, and if the medium is the message, then the requirement that rock music be loud to the point of physiological damage clearly indicates that noise is the form that creates the collectivization that does not honor the boundaries of biological integrity. At a recent concert in Amsterdam, the Irish rock group U2 was so loud that it registered as an earthquake on the seismographs at the university.

Interestingly enough, those fundamentalist ministers on television, such as the Reverend Jimmy Swaggart of Baton

Rouge, Louisiana, who rant and rave about the presence of Satan in rock music, are recognizing that there is information in what appears to be noise. Reverend Swaggart is like the Puritans of Cromwell's time who shut down all the theaters in England, for he even declaims against gospel music, but he reserves his particularly Amos-like wrath for the abominations of rock. His interpretation of what he senses is, of course, very much like the interpretations of the paranoid, a form of misplaced concreteness; but paranoia often picks up on information the normal rationalist misses. In many ways, paranoia is a response to information overload and too much noise; so it forms along with rock music the dissonance or pollution of a cybernetic society. If Don Quixote was the tragic figure of the age of print, a man whose senses were sent wandering because of the reading of books, I cannot help but see the Reverend Jimmy Swaggart as an equally tragic and quixotic figure, for he has to become a media figure to declaim against media society; but then, Amos ranted, yet he was also the first prophet to start writing his sermons. Nevertheless, Amos the shepherd did not reverse urbanization, and I doubt if the electronic evangelicals will be able to maintain the Reformation culture of what McLuhan called the "Gutenberg Galaxy" when they are bound by the same cables and constrained to become what they hate.

The rise of paranoia, from right-wing fulminations against the world conspiracy of the Trilateral Commission to Lyndon LaRouche's hatred of the British Secret Service, is an important signal that the literate, rational *citizen* of the post-Enlightenment era is being replaced by the *subject* in a shift from identity through logical definition to identity through participation and performance. In one form of consciousness, identity is seen through similar logical predicates; but in paranoia, identity is seen metaphorically as the *participation mystique* of common subjects. Looking at the erosion of good pietist values from electronic evangelical broadcasting, and looking at rock festivals, we can see that democracy is in for some hard times.

The myth of the Antichrist is that the great collectivizer unconsciously prepares for the enantiodromia, the reversal in the millennium and the mystical body of Christ. The Roman military engineers build the roads, then the missionaries use them to turn the empire into Christendom. There is a good chance that personal computers and modems could make a Swiss-style, direct participatory democracy more possible, for it is certainly true that the print technology of frequent referenda is driving the average Swiss citizen into apathy. A *de facto* representational republic is the result of the sharing of information through print in Switzerland; a *de jure* representational republic was the result of pamphleteering in the United States. However, both could be replaced by new forms of informational integration that are not as collectivizing as the hate-inciting evangelical electronic sermon or the rock concert.

Although Reverend Swaggart would like to get rid of black gospel music and white rock, it does seem to be the case that music is one of the most powerful descriptions of cultural transformation. When folk music moved from the country to the city, popular music emerged as a new cultural phenomenon. From the cotton fields of Leadbelly to the

New Orleans of Bunk Johnson, jazz is an aural history that
chronicles the transformation from agricultural to industrial
society. And from the New Orleans of Bunk Johnson to the
Chicago of Bix Beiderbecke and the Harlem of Duke Ellington is another chapter in the diaspora. The transition from
industrial to postindustrial can be seen in the breaking up
of popular music into an ecology of consciousness of incred-
ible diversity. The range of jazz forms from those of Dizzy
Gillespie to John Coltrane and Miles Davis is one expression
of a culture in which neither the melodic line nor the production line holds values together any longer. And from
rock-and-roll to acid rock was another expression that the
dominance of the middle class was at an end.

From eighteenth-century Samuel Richardson to nineteenth-century Samuel Smiles, industrial society saw the
intense effort on the part of the lower classes to take on the
culture of the middle classes. Even the aristocrat traded in
his elegant satin for the somber black of the capitalist. Gone
was the medieval diversity of tramp and tinker, artisan and
tradesman, aristocrat and soldier; arrived was the uniformity
of clerk and banker. The man of wealth was no longer an
ostentatious eighteenth-century rake, and the worker was no
longer a peasant in rags but a Bob Cratchet of Dickens's
A Christmas Carol. Furthermore, in style, the distance between rich Scrooge and poor Cratchet is not as great as the
distance between lord and laborer in preindustrial society.

Now, in our truly post industrial society, what punk music
and dress is signaling is the end of the middle class's ability
to dictate styles of taste and decorum to the social order
beneath them. Even more than that, punk dress is signaling
a sublimation of British class warfare into information. Since

political systems are often parodies of ecosystems, we can see in punk dress all the rich signaling of the animal kingdom, for the stylized *agons* of fighting rams are not fatal, and the elaborate horns are not designed for combat as much as display. And so it is with spiked hair and metal chains. The "structurally unemployed" of Thatcher's monetarist kingdom have their *agon* with the postindustrial managerial class, a class that now has no need of them whatsoever: not as slaves, not as peasants, and not as proletarians; but what the English working class has done is rather imaginative, for they have recycled the proletariat and turned it into pure art style, pure information. Noise has become potent information in the form of the global fashion and music industries, and it is appropriate that both the Chelsea School of Art and the punks arc on the King's Road. With the recent amplification of music and fashion through the new genre of music video, the size of this global industry is staggering. Considering how little the English have had to invest in the working class in the form of the dole, and remembering how much they have wasted in the arms race and in subsidizing nuclear power stations and the Concorde, the return on the investment of the dole in the post-working class is phenomenal. From records, video, film, magazines, and changing fashions of clothes, one can see that there is now a wholly new kind of parasitical media middle class feeding off the actions of the working class beneath it.

Ironically, though the young work hard to be visible, the members of Thatcher's Parliament cannot see that popular singers are now captains of industry; as once were the Josiah Wedgewoods and the Cornelius Vanderbilts, so now the Boy Georges and Michael Jacksons. Show-business Reagan, however, is more sophisticated than dowdy Thatcher, for he comes from Hollywood and recognizes Michael Jackson to be a media figurehead, and so he received Jackson at the White House like a visiting head of state. And, indeed, Michael Jackson attired in his ceremonial uniform did look like Pinochet.

And so if we look without snobbery or Margaret Thatcher's middle-class ignorance at popular music, we can see that it is signaling the emergence of a collective consciousness as the linked opposite to an elitist scientific-cybernetic culture. If music is an expression of the body politic, then perhaps it is telling us something about the possible future of Europe. If the agony of conflicting political nationalisms is turned into the *agon* of competing artistic nationalisms, then the rich diversity of Europe need not generate social chaos but merely *agon*-ic display. In the transformation of the working class into the artistic class, there is an analogy of the transformation of political nationalism into artistic nationalism in a global ecology of consciousness. If the Turks in West Germany were to take elements of Middle Eastern music to create a new popular art form, the equivalent of reggae and JuJu music, they could become, not the racistly hated underdogs, but the darlings of the West Germans. Jazz did much for the acceptance of blacks by whites in the United States, and you have to have a cultural figure like Duke Ellington before you can have a presidential candidate like Jesse Jackson. Turkish teenagers are now breakdancing on the streets of West Berlin; so perhaps the young are already signaling back that they have got the message from the kids in the Bronx and are on their way.

What all the signaling back and forth indicates is that the

social complexity and diversity of the Middle Ages has returned, ending the interval of uniformity that started with the Victorians but reached its peak in the age of conformity in the United States of the fifties. It would appear that the complexity of planetary culture, however, is more diverse even than the medieval. Its basic pattern seems to be one of highly energized oppositions: punk teenager and Chelsea pensioner, orange-suited Sanyasins and white-suited astronauts, rock stars and electronic evangelists, invisible artists such as Thomas Pynchon or the Sprayer of Zürich, and a whole parade of politicians, snake-oil salesmen, transvestites, and yuppies. With the return of the Middle Ages on the turn of the historical spiral, comes the return of the knight. Gone is the anonymous G.I. Joe of the industrial era; returned is the professional soldier, the elitist ranger, and the SWAT specialist who like a white blood cell is trained to flow through the body politic and take out assassins and terrorists.

Will this postcivilizational complexity driven by a runaway capitalism that generates ever new differences, pollution, noise, cults, and technological innovation end in a new steady state? Will it become an authoritarian state of the Greens in which individuals are not allowed to have cars and numerous possessions? Or will this postcivilization simply spawn a universal facism: a fascism of the Left in some socialist countries, a fascism of the Right in some capitalist countries, and a fascism of the Greens in ecologist countries? Or will postcivilization, in a classical enantiodromia, reverse itself to become the mystical body of Christ foreshadowed by the demonic body of Satan? That is, in fact, what McLuhan, the prophet of the electronic global village, thought:

Psychic communal integration, made possible by the electronic media, could create the universality of consciousness
foreseen by Dante when he predicted that men would continue as no more than broken fragments until they were
unified into an inclusive consciousness. In a Christian sense,
this is merely a new interpretation of the mystical body of
Christ; and Christ, after all, is the ultimate extension of
man.[26]

The world view of humanity in the Atlantic cultural
ecology was of *objects* separated in space. The world view
of humanity in the fourth cultural ecology (as experienced
by astronauts, such as Rusty Schweickart, or mystics, such
as David Spangler[27]) is of *presences* in an interpenetrating
field. How, then, do we live with this knowledge? If pollution, evil, noise, and paranoia are expressions of presences
that won't go away, how do we deal with them? Hoffman-La
Roche, even after the accident of Seveso, did not become
more responsible with dioxin; it simply hired Mannesmann
to take it away, and then Mannesmann hired a truck driver
to get rid of it. Neither Hoffman-La Roche nor Mannesmann wanted to think about dioxin; so the truck driver was
free to take the barrels and stick them in an empty shed in
a village in France. And that is typical behavior for industrial
man: objects are separated by space, and so we can have
mansions at one end and deadly poison at the other. But
when we realize that pollution is a presence, we have to
create only things we can be present with. Dioxin is a poi-
sonous side product in the creation of ugly herbicides such
as Agent Orange, and it should, very simply, never be made.
If we make such things as Agent Orange or plutonium, they
are simply not going to go away, for there is no *way* in which

to put them. If we force animals into concentration camps in feed lots, we will become sick from the antiobiotics with which we inject them; if we force nature into monocrop agribusiness, we will become sprayed by our own pesticides; if we move into genetic engineering, we will have genetic pollution; if we develop genetic engineering into evolutionary engineering, we will have evolutionary pollution. Industrial civilization never seems to learn, from DDT or thalidomide, plutonium or dioxin: catastrophe is not an accidental by-product of an otherwise good system of progress and control; catastrophe is an ecology's response to being treated in an industrial manner.

Precisely because pollution cannot go away, we must generate only those kinds of pollution we can live with. Precisely because enemies won't go away, for the fundamentalists' process of inciting hate only creates enemies without end, we have no choice but to love our enemies. The enantiomorphic polity of the future must have capitalists and socialists, Israelis and Palestinians, Bahais and Shiites, evangelicals and Episcopalians.

A monocrop of plants does violence to nature, and the pesticides give us Bhopal; a monocrop of culture does violence to human nature and gives us wars and extermination camps. Neither of the industrial operations called Buchenwald or Bhopal were accidents; they were essential descriptions of the industrial mentality, for how we treat a rock or a weed tells us how we will treat a human being in the future. Until we realize that matter is an illusion and that nature is alive, we will not be able to save our own lives from the violence we inflict all around us. If that sounds like Celtic animism, it is.

THE FOURFOLD PATTERN

Cultural Ecology

I. Riverine
II. Mediterranean
III. Atlantic
IV. Pacific-Aerospace

Economy (Marx)

I. Asiatic
II. Feudal
III. Capitalistic
IV. Socialistic

Polity

I. City-state
II. Empire
III. Industrial nation-state

IV. Enantiomorphic ?

Form of Pollution

I. Soil Loss
II. Deforestation
III. Atmospheric pollution
IV. Noise, Paranoia

Communication System (McLuhan)

I. Script
II. Alphabetic
III. Print
IV. Electronic

Mathematical Mode

I. Enumeration
II. Geometrizing
III. Equations of motion, dynamics
IV. Catastrophe theory leading to processual, multidimensional morphologies and return of mythic hieroglyphics

Archetypal Religious Leader	Religious Mode of Experience
I. Dumuzi	I. Momentary possession
II. Moses	II. Surrender to authority
III. Luther	III. Commitment to belief
IV. Group as an ecology of consciousness	IV. Symbiotic consciousness

Characteristic Good	Characteristic Evil
I. Humble piety	I. Pride, arrogant assertion of self
II. Obedience to law	II. Revolt against authority
III. Understanding of doctrine	III. Ecstatic escape or transcendence
IV. Universal compassion	IV. Collectivization through terror

Climactic Literary Masterpiece	Characteristic Cosmogonies*
I. *Gilamesh Epic*	I. *Enuma Elish*
II. Dante's *Divine Comedy*	II. Hesiod's *Theogony*
III. Joyce's *Finnegans Wake*	III. Darwin's *On the Origin of Species*
IV. ?	IV. Disney's *Fantasia*

*See note 28, page 150.

The world is now an amphictyony of nations, as once
Athens and Israel were amphictyonies of tribes. The evolution of amphictyony into polis or nation was a violent one,
and looking at Beirut or Amritsar today there is no reason
to think that the transition from an amphictyony of nations
to an enantiomorphic polity will be peaceful and rational.
But if the evil of collectivization through terror is foreshad-
owing an emergent level of historical order, then there is
some hope that humanity may actually make it from one
cultural ecology to the other.

Each cultural ecology of the past has had its landscape,
its form of pollution, its positive unconscious or *episteme*
that united literary and mathematical narratives, and its
mode of religious experience, with its characteristic way of
encountering good and evil. My purpose in composing a
historical narrative in which these patterns are put forward
is both personal and social. The personal one is to try to
understand why as a Californian I long for a real world of
culture in an imagined "back East" or in Europe, and yet
cannot really accept the narrowing of consciousness I find
in Los Angeles, New York, Toronto, London, Paris, or
Bern, Switzerland. Living in California, I imagine Europe;
now, writing this book in Europe, I reimagine the California that I grew up in. As T. S. Eliot said, "And the end of
all our exploring / Will be to arrive where we started /
And know the place for the first time." The social reason
is to hope that this narrative can make a contribution in
the movement from *mystique* to *politique* to become a
performance of the very reality it seeks to describe.

Notes

1. See Herman Kahn and Anthony Weiner, THE YEAR 2000 (New York: Macmillan, 1967), and Aubrey Burl, AVEBURY (Yale University Press: New Haven, 1980). Burl continues the intellectual traditions of Glyn Daniel and R. J. C. Atkinson in seeing the makers of Stonehenge and Avebury as superstitious savages whose life was nasty, brutish, and short. Burl ridicules Alexander Thom's studies of the complex geometries of the stone circles as a lot of nonsense, of Einstein in a sheepskin. The art historians, as opposed to the archaeologists, are much more sensitive, and sensible, in dealing with other world views. See, for example, Michael Dames's THE SILBURY TREASURE (London: Thames and Hudson, 1976) or Keith Critchlow's TIME STANDS STILL (London: Gordon Fraser, 1979). One archaeologist within a university department of archaeology who shows an art historian's sensitivity in reading imagery is UCLA's Marija Gimbutas; see her GODS AND GODDESSES OF OLD EUROPE (London: Thames & Hudson, 1974).

2. See Werner Heisenberg, "The Representation of Nature in Contemporary Physics," in SYMBOLISM IN RELIGION AND LITERATURE, ed. by Rollo May (New York: Macmillan, 1960), p. 209.

3. From Saussure to Barthes to Lévi-Strauss to Foucault to Derrida, French thinking is textual analysis. Derrida is more open to German and American thinking than most Frenchmen, but his world view is French, and his famous statement *"Il*

n'y a rien dehors textes" sums up the approach. The old, dreary battle between British empiricism and Continental rationalism lives on; the Anglo-Americans favoring perception and neorealism, the Continental Europeans favoring perception seen as the *reading* of signs and texts. The French do not take in Asian thought; so Keiji Nishitani's invocation of Dogen's "dropping off of body and mind" would be inconceivable to them. Curiously, however, Francisco Varela has been enthusiastically received in Paris, but the French tend to ignore his interest in Buddhism and read him simply as an exponent of "self-organizing systems biology," for this approach yields maps and recursive diagrams and these can be read as *texts.*

In a world city such as New York, the artist is a culture hero, for art has a commercial and marketable side to it that makes it fit in well with the life of a financial center. So artists such as Andy Warhol, Norman Mailer, Martha Graham, and Philip Glass can become influential cultural presences more than actual leaders. The thinkers, however, that New York tends to prefer are not philosophers but management consultants and gurus of marketing trends such as Alvin Toffler and John Naisbitt. Although there are literary critics and writers in the NEW YORK REVIEW OF BOOKS milieu, there are no philosophers who stand out in the way philosophers do in Paris. LE MONDE has recently published a paperback collection of its interviews with Paris's legion of thinkers (see EN-TRETIENS AVEC LE MONDE: I. PHILOSOPHIES (Paris: LE MONDE, 1984).); it is hard to imagine either the NEW YORK TIMES or the VILLAGE VOICE doing such a thing. There is, of course, a shadow side to French thinking, for much of what is simply empty posturing passes for thought. Thinking in Paris seems to be a kind of mental break-dancing in which the flashiness of the verbal moves is part of the performance. There is a code in which names are flashed (*chez* Girard, *chez* Serres), and exactly like flash cards at half time during a football game, it is not necessary to communicate the idea of an author; it is simply necessary to flash his name. Consequently, the code that signals back and forth between Parisians is fairly local; it does not necessarily have to relate to, or influence, the outside world. In this world of styles of thought as fashion, incomprehensibility is the ultimate sexiness. Clarity and straightforwardness of thought would be something seen as dowdy, plain, and obvious; a philosophical equivalent of the dress of the Queen of England.

In the old days, when culture could be stored in a book and a city, you had James Joyce's Dublin, T.S. Eliot's London, and Jean Paul Sartre's Paris. Now, in an electronic culture, in which information is not a place but a network, I find it hard to settle down. Location now seems, not a handle on culture, but a lock. So, like a medieval monk, I am always on the move, and my own style of thinking as expressed in this book cannot be defined as emanating from Los Angeles, New York, Toronto, London, Paris, Zürich, or Bern, where the book was actually written. This book will appear in a German translation in Munich before it appears in English in San Francisco. The contents of the book originated in lectures given in Findhorn, Scotland; Paris; Toronto; Rithymnon, Crete; and the University of Hawaii in Honolulu and Kyoto, Japan. All of these places have provided a life-giving atmosphere to breathe but not a soil in which to take root. I will let the reader determine what is airborne seeds and what is cultural deracination.

4. See Keiji Nishitani, RELIGION AND NOTHINGNESS (Berkeley: University of California Press, 1982), p. 285.

5. For an interesting approach to the Pacific Shift in philosophy, one that moves from Nagarjuna to Nishitani, Heidegger to Derrida, see Evan Thompson, "Planetary Thinking, Planetary Building" in the journal PHILOSOPHY EAST-WEST (Honolulu: University of Hawaii, in press).

6. See Francisco Varela's refutations of representationism in "Living Ways of Sense-Making: A Middle Path for Neuro-Science," in DISORDER AND ORDER, ed. P. Livingstone (Palo Alto: Stanford University Press, 1985). See also Humberto Maturana and Francisco Varela, EL ARBOL DEL CONOCI-MIENTO (Santiago, Chile: Editorial Universitaria, 1984), p. 89.

7. Gregory Bateson, MIND AND NATURE (New York: E. P. Dutton, 1979), p. 29.

8. Gregory Bateson, STEPS TO AN ECOLOGY OF MIND (New York: Ballantine, 1972), p. 444.

9. Russell Schweickart, "No Frames, No Boundaries," in EARTH'S ANSWER: EXPLORATIONS OF PLANETARY CULTURE AT THE LINDISFARNE CONFERENCES (New York: Harper & Row/Lindisfarne, 1977), p. 11.

10. See Bateson, STEPS TO AN ECOLOGY OF MIND, p. 432.

11. See Michel Foucault, THE ORDER OF THINGS (New York: Vintage, 1973), p. xxii.

12. See William Irwin Thompson, EVIL AND WORLD ORDER (New York: Harper & Row, 1977), p. 16.

13. See "Turner traduit Carnot" in Michel Serres, HERMES III: LA TRADUCTION (Paris: Editions de Minuit, 1974). The work of Michel Serres interests me for several reasons. First, it is a confirmation of my own approach in taking myth seriously; second, without knowing one another's works, we were making similar points in our public lectures in the seventies (though I find Serres's discussion of the Turner-Carnot relationship much better than mine); and, third, his literary approach to philosophy is an example of of the genre I have elsewhere termed *Wissenskunst* (knowledge as an art form).

14. From a talk by Gary Snyder to the Lindisfarne Fellows Gathering, Zen Center Green Gulch Farm, June 1980.

15. Immanuel Wallerstein, THE MODERN WORLD-SYSTEM, vol. 1, THE RISE OF CAPITALIST AGRICULTURE IN THE SIXTEENTH CENTURY (New York: Academic Press, 1974), p. 348.

16. See Michel Serres, HERMES V: LE PASSAGE DU NORD-OUEST (Paris: Les Editions de Minuit, 1980), p. 194. *"L'origine de la géometrie est plongée dans l'histoire sacrificielle et les deux parallèles sont désormais en connexion. La légende, le mythe, l'histoire, la philosophie, et la science pure ont des bords communs sur quoi un schéma unitaire construit des ponts."*

17. See William Irwin Thompson, THE TIME FALLING BODIES TAKE TO LIGHT (New York: St. Martin's Press, 1981), p. 96.

18. See Alexander Thom, MEGALITHIC LUNAR OBSERVATORIES (Oxford: Oxford University Press, 1971), and Dames, THE SILBURY TREASURE.

19. Kathleen Freeman, ANCILA TO THE PRE-SOCRATICS (Cambridge, MA: Harvard University Press, 1962), p. 19.

20. See Samuel Noah Kramer and Diane Wolkstein, INANNA: QUEEN OF HEAVEN (New York: Harper and Row, 1983).

21. See Thompson, THE TIME FALLING BODIES TAKE TO LIGHT, p. 167.

22. Claude Lévi-Strauss, "The Structural Study of Myth," in STRUCTURAL ANTHROPOLOGY (New York: Basic Books, 1963), p. 58.

23. Julian Jaynes, THE ORIGINS OF CONSCIOUSNESS IN THE BREAKDOWN OF THE BICAMERAL MIND (Boston: 1976).

24. The best refutation of the simplistic thinking of the correlation of states of consciousness to physical location in the brain is in Humberto Maturana and Francisco Varela's AUTOPOESIS AND COGNITION, Boston University Studies in the Philosophy of Science (Bordrecht, Holland: Reidl and Co., 1980),

vol. 42. Varela has also elaborated his own approach in his PRINCIPLES OF BIOLOGICAL AUTONOMY (New York: Elsevier-Holland, 1979).

25. Erich Kahler, THE TOWER AND THE ABYSS (New York: Praeger, 1956).

26. Marshall McLuhan, interview, PLAYBOY, March 1969.

27. The postreligious spirituality of New Age thinkers such as David Spangler is interpreted by Christian fundamentalists as the Antichrist, and on the Christian cable television channel in the United States, David Spangler and Marilyn Ferguson have been singled out for abusive caricatures of their religious beliefs. The shrillness of Constance Cumby's paranoid declamations should be compared with the quiet, sane, and unpretentious tone of David Spangler's new book EMERGENCE: THE REBIRTH OF THE SACRED (New York: Dell, 1984).

28. The narratives we tell about the creation of the universe and the origin of life tell us about the articulation of order within a specific cultural ecology. For the Riverine cultural ecology, as expressed in the Babylonian ENUMA ELISH, the unfoldment of the world is a movement from the prehistoric Great Mother to the historic Great Father, from chaos to polis, from entropy to order in the power of the word. This Babylonian archetypal narrative can be seen lurking behind works as different as Genesis or Aeschylus's ORESTEIA. The male consort to the Great Mother is seen to be a particularly horrible abomination to the masculine hero of the new patriarchal order. Kingu is abominable to Marduk in much the same way that Aegisthus is abominable to Agamemnon and Orestes. This is a historic vestige of the old prehistoric conflict between the mother's brother of matrilineal society and the father of patrilineal society. The ORESTEIA is also similar to the ENUMA ELISH in that it, too, is a narrative of cosmic unfoldment from chaos to polis in which the female is seen to be dark, bloody, and regressive, whereas the male is seen

to be light, rational, and progressive. The Babylonian poem ends with a celebration of the city; the Greek poem ends with a celebration of the law courts of Athens. The isomorphisms between the two works are fascinating, but since Greek artisans worked on the temples of Persepolis, we should realize that people and ideas traveled more in the Old World than we are in the habit of recognizing.

The basic cosmogonic narrative for the Atlantic cultural ecology is, of course, Darwin's; but to be fair to precursors, I should point out that Robert Chambers's VESTIGES OF CREATION was really the earlier mythic narrative of evolution, and it preceded ON THE ORIGIN OF SPECIES by fifteen years, for it was published in London in 1844.

Lest literary intellectuals of the Atlantic epoch rush to attack me for listing Walt Disney's FANTASIA alongside Hesiod's THEOGONY and Darwin's ORIGIN, let me be quick to say that I am not claiming that it is intellectually or artistically equal to them. I am saying that in its vision of evolution wed to classical music, it is prophetic of a visualization of thinking that I believe is going to replace the literate sensibility of the "Gutenberg Galaxy," and that its mythologizing of the previous scientific narratives of evolution is characteristic of a postmodernist sensibility in which myth and science are combined. From the point of view of this post modernist consideration of myth, Michel Serres's work, my own THE TIME FALLING BODIES TAKE TO LIGHT and BLUE JADE FROM THE MORNING STAR, and Philip Glass's score for KOYAANISQATSI and AKHNATON are all expressions of a new sensibility. Whether one wishes to label this "postmodernist" or "New Age" is a matter of affiliation to different subcultures. The subscribers to THE NEW YORK REVIEW OF BOOKS use the term "postmodernist"; the subscribers to RESURGENCE or NEW AGE JOURNAL prefer the implicit chiliasm of "New Age."

CHAPTER

Gaia
Politique

When the adaptive play of a mentality
reaches the point of its climactic growth within a cultural
ecology, the imagination surrounds the old mentality, rearticulates it in an intense fashion that amounts to a miniaturization, and then moves on into the larger space of the
unknown. The genius consummates and finishes a mentality
and takes us to the borders of the new cultural ecology; but
like Moses on Mount Pisgah, the genius can often see the
Promised Land, yet is not able, or is not permitted, to enter
it. So it is that a genius such as James Joyce can bring us to
the end of the Atlantic epoch and the linguistic edge of
literature in *Finnegans Wake,* but cannot pass over into the
hieroglyphic thinking of an electronic age; so it is that a
Wittgenstein or a Heidegger can bring us to the end of a
world picture, but cannot create the new world view. What
Jean Francois Lyotard calls *"les petits récits"*[1] of postmodernism now follow the grand recitals of Darwin, Marx, and
Freud. Nowadays European intellectuals go around and

around again over the same ground, like bloodhounds that have lost the scent, but the fugitive imagination has escaped into Buddhist groundlessness. Numberless are the intellectuals who try to play Sartre in the cafes of Paris, numberless are the Marxists in West Germany who try to replace the world with a system; but there is no living imagination left in these Xeroxes of a Xerox. Try as the Europeans may, they cannot become the architects of a grand new edifice of thought, for the new cultural ecology is not exclusively an edifice of thought; it is more a mystical spirituality incarnated in the context of aerospace and cybernetic technologies. It is not that the European intellectual, whether a Habermas of the Left or a Voegelin of the Right, is not intelligent enough to understand, for intelligence is his or her genius; it is more simply that the intellectual is not open to the imagination of novelty and instinctively rejects what would threaten the world as he or she *knows* it. Small wonder that feminists and Zen monks, rock stars and computer hackers, citizen activists and artistic entrepreneurs have hijacked Europe and taken it to California.

It is not that an archaic mysticism is superior to Habermas's "Reason," but rather that a Zen "dropping off of body and mind" allows both mind and body the imaginative freedom with which to reincarnate themselves within the mentality appropriate for the fourth cultural ecology. In the process of cultural miniaturization, preindustrial forms of spirituality, such as animism, yoga, and Zen, are themselves surrounded and compressed by the imagination, and the popular interest in shamanism, psychic channeling, and the occult is an indication of their passing away. Like the explosion of interest in the Hermetic tradition that came in the

Renaissance, from Ficino to Paracelsus to John Dee, the current revival of interest in the occult in the West is a sign that the psychic level of consciousness, just as much as the ratiocinative and conceptual level of consciousness, is about to be broken down, digested, and absorbed within a new mentality that is neither irrational nor merely rational.

Like an infant that knows what it needs and can point to food, even though it cannot define it, one can gesture and shake one's head in negation more easily than one can conceptually define a new cultural ecology when we have only just entered it. Since this new mentality could last for a very long time, it would be silly to think that one could define it now; but one can shake one's head when the old is proposed as the new, and so I shake my head in negation at both Habermas and Rajneesh.

Even though I am an intellectual with a European turn of mind, and even though I am the scholar-in-residence at the Episcopal Cathedral in New York, I do not believe that this new mentality is what we know as academic or religious. When I encounter a culture like that of the Hopi, where there is no religion but where the whole way of life is sacred, I tend to think that the future will be more like that: not sacerdotal, but sacred; not institutional, but universal. Imagine a life like that of the traditional Hopi lived in an environment of aerospace technologies and micro-electronics that permit the machines to be, not large, industrial, and threatening to the trees, but small, tuned to a different scale, and symbiotic with living things. No simple regression to the pre-industrial past could bring this about, and no Marxist-Leninist revolution, in which nature and the differentiated society are violently transformed into a condition of scientific socialism, could bring this about either. Marxism is a system of industrial thinking, a patriarchal vision of the domination of nature by culture; romanticism is a form of anti-industrial thinking, a vision of the feminine dominance of nature over culture. The meta-industrial culture I have discussed before is neither the one nor the other.[2]

One can tell a good deal about a work of art or philosophy by the critics it attracts; so the fact that the view that I am presenting has been attacked by East Coast neoconservatives as being feminist, and at the same time has been attacked by feminists as being fascist (because of its mysticism), appeals to my Irish sense of whimsy.[3] The fashionable critic is always a bastion of defense of the old paradigm, of the old mentality in which he or she has achieved that position of success; but the critics kill what they love, for they reduce the mentality they copy and are more like Xerox machines of received opinion than artistic creators of novelty. The critic defends the geniuses of the past from the charlatans and lunatics of the present, but ultimately nothing is left of the vividness and life with which a genius first created or consummated a mentality. Ironically, the unschooled are often more sensitive to the new than a critic in a prestigious journal or a professor in a university. The genius may move on, but the follower of a counterculture experiences a dislocation. Yet, in many cases, the solitary genius and the collective subculture feel alienated from an elite and its preferred ancestral culture; so the first step in moving on into a new future is to look back to set up a different ancestral culture.

The desire to look back and replace the Romans and the

Greeks with a different ancestral culture is not new, for each generation sets up the horizon of its consciousness with an ancestral culture from which it takes its new identity. Ficino and Gemisthos Plethon set down the Romans and set up the Greeks. The Romantics set up the northern European gods, and Yeats in particular set up the Celts as the counterculture to the imperium, Roman or English. Today the New Age romantics are more planetary in their archaic celebrations, for they are attracted to native American Indians, Tibetan Buddhists, the civilization of ancient Egypt, and the megalithic cultures of Western Europe; but they are never attracted to the Romans, for in their mystical quest for other dimensions of meaning, it is precisely a society of soldiers, statesmen, and engineers that they are trying to escape. Whatever is missing in materialistic, industrial society is certainly not to be found in the Roman Empire.

The dislocation of consciousness from civilization is experienced by everyone except the fashionable critics and the academic philosophers, for they must hold to precisely those definitions of culture that sustain their identity and their positions of affluence and influence. Like churchmen in the age of Galileo, it is not humanly possible for them to imagine what the new world will do to old Europe. But not all of this conservatism is bad, and some of it is certainly a healthy resistance to seizures of hysteria. Much of what pretends to be New Age is simply a rejection of modernism and bourgeois democracy in a longing for the hierarchically ordered world of imaginary ancient theocracies. René Guenon preferred Islam, Schwaller de Lubicz preferred ancient Egypt, and Alain Dánelieu prefers Shivite India[4]; but all three are similar in their reactionary abhorrence of secular democracy. Thus the Jean Elshtains and Christopher Lasches, or the Conor Cruise O'Briens and Fritz Raddatzes who guard the portals to the temple of modernism do serve as watchdogs who bark and snip at all these romantic lunatics and devotees who seek to drag us back into the theocracy, the caste system, or the satrapy of some megalomaniacal guru.

We cannot go back, and the New Age is supposed to be new and not old; but much of what passes for New Age in America, England, and West Germany is simply the psychic rubble of lost civilizations. It may be fun for Americans and Americanized West Germans to wear turbans and dress like twelfth century mullahs, or to wear an orange uniform and hang oneself with the noose of a guru around one's neck, or to renounce phlegm-producing dairy products in a gnostic's horror of *Mater* and milk to have Japanese miso soup for breakfast, for these kinds of cross-cultural play have been going on in the West since the Crusades; it only becomes serious and deadly when the elect tramp through the protective swamp that separates religion from politics. When living people become the dolls that are manipulated in the child's fantasy play of Masters of The Universe, then it becomes critical to keep play within the limits of conscience and compassion. Thus, sarcastic critics who pour out their icy contempt on the anointed heads of the gurus are actually providing a critical public-health service in the life of the polis.

William Blake said, "In opposition is true friendship,"

Third Cultural Ecology	*Fourth Cultural Ecology*
• Print	• Electronics
• Greek abstraction	• Neo-Egyptian hieroglyphic thinking
• Identity through definition by logical predicates	• Identity as *participation* mystique of subjects in Whiteheadian "prehensive unification"
• Ego defined by possessions	• *Daimon* experienced as topological synchrony, diachronic performance
• Civilization embodied in a world city	• Planetary culture as participation in a moving process or network
• Routinization through commerce and economics	• Routinization through ecology and Gaian forms of "planet management"[5]
• Creative disequilibrium and rapid change	• Steady state and consolidation into form
• Technological clutter and gigantic buildings and machines	• Technological minimalism and miniaturization; technologies that mimic organic processes
• *Homo faber*	• *Homo ludens*
• Industrial nation-state	• Enantiomorphic polity
• Evil as inflicted death and suffering	• Evil as controlled life and deferred death; torture through the breakdown of the personality by electronic stimulation of the pleasure centers of the brain (ESB); a shift from natural living to biomedical processing.

and "Without contraries is no progression"; so critical opposition provides two functions in the complex life of the body politic: first, the critics kill what they love by defending the old elite, thus helping to break down and digest the old rigid institutions; second, they improve the genetic quality of the New Age by removing the cult from culture.

Every individual is an ecology of opposites within himself or herself, and so in loving one's enemy, one gains compassion and an understanding of oneself. These paradoxes are evident in the very substance of this book, for in content's cosmetic disguise of structure, this book about the Pacific Shift has been written in Europe and is a European intellectual attempt *to think out* the implications of the new cultural ecology in the words and terms of the old cultural ecology. What Bateson, Nishitani, Varela, and I all share is not simply a Pacific orientation, but a European philosophical background. Equally paradoxical is the fact that in responding to critics such as Raddatz or Elshtain, I, too, must play the role of critic and not mystic or artist; but were I to succeed in demolishing the critics of the New Age or the postmodernist mythopoeic mentality, I too would kill what I love as the New Age drowned in a swamp of mindlessness.

So, to continue in this vein of the acceptance of paradox, I think it would be timely to be categorical about the noncategorical and descriptive of the indescribable to express the movement from one mentality to another *in* the old mentality of lists and definitions. If, as I believe, Europe has been finished by its great geniuses, what then is in this movement from the third cultural ecology to the fourth?

I could go on, but the pattern would basically repeat itself, for the pattern expresses the limits to my own imagination. Whether one sees the next culture in terms of Yeats's "antithetical gyre," or Gunther Stent's "coming of the golden age and the end of Progress,"[6] the basic intuition is that a shift from industrial work, abstraction, and materialism to play, sensual consciousness, and an unimaginable culture will, no doubt, be quite different from Yeats's aristocracy or Stent's polynesia. Whatever content this culture will have, its coming involves a transformation as large as the one from medievalism to modernism, and perhaps even as large as the one from Paleolithic to Neolithic. I would like to emphasize, however, that I do not see this transformation as a utopian one in which evil is eliminated for good. Marx prophesied that with the achievement of communism, "the prehistory of mankind would be at an end," but I think the elimination of evil will require more than a classless, undifferentiated society; rather, it will require something closer to the Buddha's "Enlightenment of all sentient beings," and that may take a little while longer than a Platonic month of 2160 years.

The most immediate political danger in our era of transition is the loss of the consciousness of the individual mind through terror and collectivization. The individual consciousness is the unique that contributes to the human race's evolutionary universal; evil is the anti-evolutionary force that crushes spirit, mind, and body into the unit in the uniform mass. The unique vitalizes differences, but the unit smashes them, and that is why the ego-reduction techniques of totalitarian states and contemporary cults can be classed as evil.

Brandon's speculations?

but not that of Zen or Christianity (see Merton)

Even if humanity were to become a single being, as described by Arthur C. Clarke in his science-fiction novel *Childhood's End*, it is important to remember that the individual can only contribute to the formation of a more cosmic Mind *by being a mind*. Techniques that destroy the integrity of the mind, therefore, would prevent, by definition, the emergence of just such a cosmic Mind. An organelle within a cell, such as a chloroplast or a mitochondrion, can contribute to the life of a cell by converting sunlight into sugar or by producing oxygen; if it ceases to hold its unique ability, it ceases to be an evolutionary symbiont. Human beings, even when mentally retarded or senile, still have the ability to convert matter into consciousness, light into language; consequently, in religious societies in which human consciousness is the basic value (as opposed to industrial productivity), the aged and the infirm are felt to be part of the social conscience and consciousness. It is precisely this kind of recognition of the reality of consciousness that I see as being basic to the foundation of any future polity. In Bateson's terms, Mind is immanent in nature; it is not epiphenomenal to matter. The "difference that makes a difference" between love and hate is that love affirms difference, whereas hate crushes it. The narcissist can love only himself as he is reflected in things and persons who are constrained to be clones of himself; but in a state of compassion, one is capable of expanding one's awareness by learning and by accepting difference. Jesus's counsel to love one's enemy is, therefore, not sentimental slop, but an affirmation of the process of differentiation upon which life is based. Anything else is dangerous and, in our era, even genocidal.

There are, of course, a lot of people on television these days talking about Jesus and politics; so we need to continue our appreciation of difference by making a few distinctions. Jesus also said, "By their fruits, ye shall know them," and warned that there would be so many false prophets around that one would have to learn how to tell them apart. So, if an evangelist on television is inciting people to hate, then hate is the fruit of his or her ministry. If the evangelist is dividing up the population into those who are acceptable in "the eyes of the Lord" (meaning his or her own eyes), and if suddenly teenagers and black gospel singers are seen to be worthy of abhorrence, then, clearly, the ministry is trying to teach us how to hate so that we can "purify" society by crushing all difference into the uniformity of the "saved" congregation. Jews, Catholics, and the fallen must be "converted." The fruits of this kind of ministry are anything but love and a compassionate acceptance of one's enemies.

Precisely because I see the recognition of differences as the consciousness of the unique that contributes to the understanding of the universal, I do not see the noetic polity of the future as an authoritarian state, and I would strongly disagree with those scholars, such as Schwaller de Lubicz, Alain Dánelieu, and Robert Lawlor,[7] who celebrate ancient theocracies and caste systems as the form of society that is appropriate for a mystically enlightened civilization. The cultural evolution of the individual, as championed by such writers as William Blake, Thomas Jefferson, and Walt Whitman, has been to a point, and to bring that historical vision of democracy and individual rights to the point of this particular book, I would like to conclude with a consideration of how the Pacific Shift may affect the cultural movement from philosophy to polity, from *mystique* to *politique*.

At the present time, Gaia is more of a mythos than an idea; it is a symbolic complex in which various individuals and groups participate without necessarily having the same scientific definition of the planet as a self-regulating living system. Historically, Gaia is the Greek name for the Mother Earth Goddess, celebrated in the Homeric hymns and in Hesiod's *Theogony:* "First of all there came Chaos / and after him came / Gaia of the broad breast, / to be the unshakable foundation / of all the immortals who keep the crests / of snowy Olympos."[8] The more recent invocation of the ancient goddess in the form of the Gaia Hypothesis comes from the fact that when the atmospheric chemist James Lovelock was going for a walk in Cornwall with his neighbor, the novelist William Golding, he discussed his recent findings about the autoregulation of the earth as a living system and asked Golding for a name for this new hypothesis. "Why not call it Gaia?" was Golding's response. From there the Gaia Hypothesis was jointly articulated in a collaboration of Lovelock and the cellular biologist Lynn Margulis. Stewart Brand helped their work to reach a wider audience by publishing an essay on the Gaia Hypothesis in *Co-Evolution Quarterly* in 1975. In 1981 it was my turn, and at that time I brought Lovelock and Margulis to meet with Stewart Brand and all the other Lindisfarne Fellows for our annual gathering.[9] From that meeting, Paul Winter's jazz mass *Missa Gaia* was inspired; it was later performed at the Cathedral of Saint John the Divine in New York and, since then, in various cities around the country. And so it is fair to say that Gaia as a mythos moves from artist to scientist to artist to citizen as it is reinvoked in the context of contemporary culture.[10] Now Gaia is being invoked by social critics such as Kirkpatrick Sale,[11] so if Péguy is right when he says that *"Tout commence en mystique et finit en politique,"* then it would seem that we are now in the period when the Weberian routinization of charisma will translate Gaia into politics and new forms of satellite resource management that are appropriate for the planetary culture of the global ecology.[12]

Gaia is as good a name as any for this new context that now surrounds the nations of the world and the institutions of industrial society. As mythos and idea, Gaia expresses the planetary ecology and artistic cultures in which the nations are seen not simply as units of production and defense, but as contributors to new modes of regional identity. As we evolve into a planetary culture, we devolve into more deeply rooted and less abstract forms of nationhood.

The industrial nation-state is a product of nineteenth-century forms of technology and thinking. The railroad helped to consolidate regions into nations in a simple imperial lattice of center and periphery, but now with communications satellites and electronics, the industrial nation-state is losing its *raison d'être*, for it is not large enough to be planetary in spirit and not small enough to be politically nourishing of civic involvement. In the nineteenth century, the industrial nation-state made economics the governing science of society and tried to produce a definition of culture through the structures of war and trade. Movements of romantic nationalism tried to challenge these definitions with forms of identity, and such leaders as Daniel O'Connell in Ireland, Louis Riel in Canada, and the Mahdi in the Sudan set the tribes against the empire. And in our own American railroad nation-state, the Ghost Dance of the Sioux pitted the spirit against the machine. These movements never disappeared, for the unstructuring of the colonial empires of Europe after World War II was the fruition of these earlier nineteenth-century forms of romantic nationalism. Now there is again much talk of nations within nations, and if devolution in Scotland and separatism in Quebec have not been carried out, it is precisely because devolution cannot be carried out in a context of national economics. Regional devolution is part of planetary evolution; so it is the larger entity that nourishes the emergence of the smaller identity. When ecology has replaced economics as the governing science of society, and when the ecological problems of transnational areas are dealt with honestly, then the Greens' call for a "Europe of the regions" or Kirkpatrick Sale's celebration of bioregionalism will be more of a political possibility.

The imperial mode of being, expressed in the myth of Ouranos, is to enforce a definition of time and space onto the present, to abort all change and emergence, and to force everything into sameness: a world of McDonald's and Coca-Cola, or a world of soldiers and secret police. But in the ancient Greek myth the children of Gaia rise up together and take away the power and potency of Ouranos so that all the different gods may emerge into the light.

The children of Gaia took power away from the old Paleolithic Ouranos with the help of the new agricultural technology, the sickle of the crescent moon that was symbolic of woman's mysteries and was used by the women in gathering wild grasses. Now, once again, the children of Gaia use a new technology against an old culture, but this time it is the aerospace and electronic technologies that take power away from the imperium of Ouranos. These new technologies of information gathering enable the gods to come out of the womb into the light.

The mythopoeic mode of perception that is the postmodernist sensibility associated with Gaia recognizes that nations are more like gods than like regional markets. Rudolph Steiner liked to talk about "folk souls," but given the Nazi exploitation of this mythic mode, most Germans today shiver in dread of some new kind of nativistic fascism rising up to challenge the sane world of industrial materialism. That would be very prudent if it were the case that all myth and mysticism were inherently fascist; but it is hard to throw William Blake, Walt Whitman, W. B. Yeats, and a Hopi elder all into the same category, and it is hard to defend the world of rationalization as sane when we see the devastation of cultures and ecologies everywhere. The mythic mode of perception often recognizes precisely the kind of information that a rationalist mentality selectively ignores. The abstract mentality is capable of transforming a tall-grass prairie into a monocrop and then holding it in place by the forces of chemical warfare against nature; it is capable of creating concentration camps for animals and holding them in place with injections that later in the food chain attack our own immunological systems; and all the time this mentality is at work, it keeps talking about reason and progress. And when

Roszak's student
essays on 60's –
Revolt in the
Where is the
resistance in the
90's? X Generation
& age passivity &
Electro pessimism
consumerism

the social designers of institutions move from feed lots to
universities, they herd the students together in a similar
fashion, but because humans are more advanced than cattle,
our students are perfectly capable of administering the drugs
to themselves on their own. This world we call reasonable
and free, but the world of myth, poetry, and spirituality the
critics call fascist.

The materialist denigration of all forms of spirituality as
fascist will not work any longer. It is an act of cultural
thievery that robs people of religious and artistic traditions
of great value. The materialist, be he capitalist or socialist,
has made a mess of matter far worse than any allegedly
otherworldly mystic. The Gaian mode of consciousness
recognizes that science, just as much as art, has a mythopoeic quality to its narratives, and as an ecological mode of
consciousness, it recognizes that opposites can coexist.

To take power away from Ouranos and give it to the
children of Gaia, one has to understand myth and poetry
and not take the metaphor literally in a paranoid's seizure
of "misplaced concreteness." Disarmament is the literal way
in which the violent pacifist seeks to castrate the military-
industrial-university complex. Small wonder that disarmament hasn't worked and that the weapons have grown in
greater numbers as the demonstrations have increased. The
demonstrator frightens the citizen with visions of thermonuclear war, but so does the general; both of them feed off fear
and both create a power base for themselves through the
terrorizing of populations. Asking the generals to disarm in
a theatrical exercise that is aimed at antagonizing the other
side and affirming one's own elect political identity is not a

true exercise in compassion and disarmament. It is more like the cultural situation in which the Pope gives a sermon from his throne on the virtues of poverty, for since the medium is the message, the context comforts the rich, while the message comforts the poor: but nothing is changed, and the rich and the poor continue in their game of opposition.

A civilian space program is a much more effective way of lifting up, negating, and transforming the arms race. And although Rudolph Bahro, the Green political theorist in West Germany, has called for the abandoning of all research and development in an attempt to go back to the ecology of a pre-industrial society, this kind of talk only helps the Christian Democrats claim that the new decentralists are the new Pol Pot social theoreticians of West Germany.

When Jerry Brown was governor of California, he tossed off an idea in a conversation with me that he never seems to have developed. In 1978 he said that if every year 5 percent of the American and Soviet defense budgets were to be transferred to a program for the joint exploration of space, and if every year an additional 5 percent were to be added to the joint space program, we could begin to build down the military budgets without throwing the American and Soviet defense industries into a state of shock. Clearly, if a peace candidate were to announce an intention to disarm overnight, the global corporations and the labor unions would be the first to eliminate the threat to their survival coming from any such peace candidate or peace movement. It is not enough to be against something; one has to be for something else. And since the space program gives us the means to see the earth as a whole, and the satellites allow

us to monitor deforestation in the Amazon Basin, the death
of the Mediterranean, or the illicit transport of nuclear
materials, it is obvious that the aerospace technologies, along
with the global forms of communication, are a strategic part
of the Gaia Politique.

There is, of course, an appropriate scale to all technological enterprise, and a transnational space program should
have as its purpose three goals: (1) mutual security as a way
of obviating the need for more expensive forms of mutual
defense,[13] (2) a more intelligent means of global resource
management and conservation, and (3) the development of
planetary forms of communication and expression for the
national and tribal cultures of the earth.

As a trans-national space program began to embody a
Gaia Politique for the planet, I think we would find that
nations would not disappear, though old nations, such as
Wales or the land of the Basques, might indeed reappear.
Abstract and merely rationalized *definitions* of nationhood
might wither as more deeply rooted national *identities*
began to emerge, like dandelions coming up through the
pavement. I do not think these identities, would be simply
romantic and restricted to folk art; national styles of scientific activity would begin to emerge and become as distinct
as national styles of literature, music, and cuisine are now.
Even at the present time, Swiss satellites, German space
labs, and Canada's arm for the space shuttle are beginning
to express, not global homogenization, but distinct cultural
approaches to technology. With a more angelic vision of
H.G. Wells's "Wings Over the World,"[14] instead of Reagan's *Star Wars,* the nations, as children of Gaia, could
begin to break away from the tyranny of Ouranos.

The space program, in a more pacific shift of the defense budget of the U.S.S.S.R., could also be helpful in the shift from economic to ecological values. In the industrial definition of human culture, the poor become "the unemployed," and the nations with few resources and no technology become the "least developed countries" that struggle to maintain their self-respect by buying into inappropriate technologies. Quite recently, however, the punks in London have generated an informational economy that dramatizes how "structural unemployment" can be transformed into art style, and the deeply indebted nations seem about to transform the economic system of the world into a global shadow economy that alters the nature of banking. First we had a punk working class; we may now be about to have punk nations. As the United States, with its trillion-dollar deficit, soon joins the line of indebted nations, the abstract definitions of the world economic system are no longer going to describe the life of the new global cultural ecology.

Hitherto, "economic development" has simply meant making loans to ruling elites in countries to enable them to destroy village agriculture so that a global agribusiness could be consolidated in the hands of large landowners, who, in turn, cooperate with their North American counterparts by buying American and Canadian tractors and chemicals. Since this system is not working very well in the San Joaquin Valley, it is certainly not going to work any better in the Punjab.

With the reduction of funds spent on the arms race, the space program could be oriented toward dealing with the global food crisis, and the satellite reconaissance of global resources could provide more intelligent means of dealing with problems such as the Greenhouse Effect, acid rain, deforestation, soil loss, and the poisoning of rivers, seas, oceans, and continental water tables. In addition, a percentage of the defense budgets could be allocated to the resource nations. Funds could be used to help nations such as Chad establish bioregional study centers that could develop into world universities that produce wealth and knowledge. As it stands now, poor nations simply export their trees to Japan and their students to Stanford and Berkeley.

Recently Jane Jacobs has argued that it is cities, and not nations, that produce wealth, and that regions without cities stay forever locked into rural poverty and resource economies[15]; but this argument is a regress ad infinitum, for if cities colonize their periphery, they become simply empires in miniature. Looking at cities such as Mexico City and Sao Paolo, and looking at M.I.T. and Route 128, the Stanford Industrial Park, and the Research Triangle of North Carolina, it seems more accurate to say that cities with world universities are the producers of wealth that serve to lift up a depressed area to connect it with a planetary economy of information. It would be difficult to give Chad an M.I.T. overnight, but it would not be difficult to establish a bioregional resource institute that could involve rural herdspeople, citydwellers, anthropologists, and ecologists in the process of dealing with the desertification that leads to famine. No doubt, Ivan Illich would see this as simply a process in which an international jet-setting class flies around to meetings, from UNEP in Nairobi to the UN in New York, but these bioregional study centers could become the rural liberal arts colleges of the new planetary culture. Distasteful as that might be to Illich's Tolstoyan love of the world's peasantry, it is not possible to stop time and keep people in the symbolic condition of peasanthood that so appeals to the divided sensibilities of such literary intellectuals as Illich, D. H. Lawrence, and W. B. Yeats. Without a complete collapse of the world economy and a recession into a new Dark Age, it is impossible to go back to a preindustrial culture or remain at the level of an industrial one. The nineteenth-century land grant legislation in the United States helped establish regional land grant colleges, and now some of these institutions, such as Cornell, have grown into world universities. Looking at Ithaca, New York, I cannot help but think that that is a better fate for Gondar, Ethiopia, than the one it now faces.

Since the post–World War II visions of economic development have clearly not worked, and since the arms race has created an American deficit that is being financed by the Third World, a new program of Third World development managed from outer space will obviously be no better than one managed from Washington or Geneva. Bioregional study centers and institutes would, therefore, need to be more like New England town meetings in which local controls were wed to global communications of the kind already being worked out by Donella Meadows at Dartmouth.[16] Whether they function like Granges of farmers or labor unions of workers or Gaian communities of people "thinking globally but acting locally" will, no doubt, vary from region to region, according to the specific cultural situations affected by such irrational imponderables as graft, drugs, and sloth; but no matter how frustrating these new situations

will be, they will not be as bad as what we have now with
the arms race perversely feeding the global famine. At the
present time, resource nations are economically forced to
trash their ecologies to promote foreign exchange, and since
the foreign exchange tends to end up in the hands of a small,
landowning elite, the flight of capital from Central America
to Miami only encourages guerilla warfare and the trashing
of traditional cultures. This, in turn, stimulates new American investments in armaments, and so it goes on into a black
hole at the speed of darkness.

A Gaia Politique will not eliminate evil from the face of
the earth, and it is important to realize that a frustrated
idealism can too easily turn into bitterness; so one needs to
work for cultural transformation with the patience of Irish
monks in the Dark Ages who knew that they would not live
to see the results of their work in the expressions of medieval
Christendom.

Although environmental engineers are trying to map out
"ecosystems" with the interpretative mechanisms borrowed
from econometrics, one will need visual imagery of much
greater richness and complexity than inputs, outputs, and
feedback loops. An *eco-logos* cannot be understood in the
terms of the old imperial maps of center and periphery or
the Cartesian grid of economic abstractions. Myth, metaphor, and poetic visual imagery come closer to the living
reality, but I trust that the scientific imagination is capable
of growth and that the Gaia Hypothesis that holds the life
of the organelles within the cell and the continents and
oceans within the atmosphere in a single vision of the biosphere is already part of that cultural transformation.

Just as the Cartesian grid and the algebraic notation of dynamics helped to develop the mentality of abstraction that was appropriate to the spread of industrial capitalism and scientific socialism, so now the recursive simultaneities of self-organizing systems biology are providing the narrative elements for the development of a new world view. It remains for some mathematical genius to integrate these narrative elements, as once Leibniz and Newton integrated the narratives of dynamics with calculus. My Irish druid radar leads me to suspect that this change will not come about within the Eurocentric conceptions of the old world view or within the limitations of our present simplistic computer languages. I suspect that when the Chinese enter the new Pacific cultural ecology with the fullness of presence now characteristic of the Japanese, they will most likely be the ones to imagine new forms of iconic, visual computer languages to turn European catastrophe theory into computer-animated, narrative, processual morphologies that will be available to all through video discs. But this is simply an Irish hunch and not a Missouri demonstration.[17]

It also remains for some political genius to play the role of a Thomas Jefferson to show how these ecological narratives are descriptive of a new kind of polity. This New Enlightenment, with its new enlightened polity, will probably be the work of the twenty-first century, for we seem doomed to be the last generation of industrial devastation and religious hysteria. Nevertheless, it is still possible to sketch an outline of what such a political theory would need to look like.

Thomas Jefferson inherited a world view shaped by what

McLuhan has called the "Gutenberg Galaxy" of literate
culture, the concept of matter in space shaped by Newtonian physics, and the concept of property in the Commonwealth articulated by John Locke. Following on Locke's
refutation of the divine right of kings, Jefferson worked to
transform the colonies of a monarchy into a republic. Because he thought in the terms of the physics of his day, he
designed a "state" that was a system of "checks and balances" of countervailing "forces." Because he saw agriculture as the basic social activity, he thought in terms of
"property" as the basis of individual "rights." Rights, of
course, were a quintessential expression of the "Gutenberg
Galaxy," so that it is not unfair to say that rights are writs.
For Locke, these rights had to do with the social foundation
of property, and property was essentially that which had
been taken out of a state of nature by labor:

> We see in *Commons,* which remain so by compact that 'tis
> the taking any part of what is common and removing it out
> of the state Nature leaves it in, *which begins the Property;*
> without which the Common is of no use.[18]

The air we breathe is certainly common to all humanity
and is "an unalienable right" without which no human
being can remain alive. The air is the last remaining part of
the historical Commons; but if now, through productive
labor, one takes the air out of a state of nature and turns it
into a poison, one has not created "property," one has actually destroyed the life, livelihood, and agricultural property
of others. For Locke and Jefferson, labor produces property,
and the rights of property generate the "Commonwealth."

For Adam Smith, Jefferson's contemporary, "the invisible hand" of the providential accountant would always balance the columns in the social ledgers to make certain that individual greed would add up to common wealth, as the factories of the nation produced riches for the owners of property and jobs for the workers. From seventeenth-century Locke and Newton, through eighteenth-century Smith and Jefferson, to twentieth-century Thatcher, Reagan, and Kohl, the industrial world view is taken for granted as being a description of reality in which objects are "simply located" in vacant, containing space, and both people and objects are seen as property simply located in the vacant, containing space of the state of nature. Neither objects nor people are seen as *presences* in an interpenetrating field, and so we take it for granted that we can have pleasant homes safely separated from toxic dumps in our Commonwealth.

To move out of the simpler world of Adam Smith's eighteenth century or Karl Marx's nineteenth century, substitute electronics for the "Gutenberg Galaxy," self-organizing systems biology for Newtonian physics, and ecology for economics as the dominant narratives of cultural transactions. Labor created value in the production of property for Locke, but in our informational society property is no longer simply land; it is consciousness. Following the insights of Gregory Bateson, we can see that "matter" is not the state of nature, but that the pathways of information extend outside the body and that Mind is immanent in nature; therefore, the "state of nature" is not wild land, as it was for Locke, but unconscious Mind, or Gaia. For our cybernetic age, to take property out of a state of nature means to lift consciousness

out of Mind by the labor of thinking or meditation. Mind
is basic to nature, and consciousness is basic to humanity,
for as I have said before, even the retarded and the senile
have the basic capacity of transforming light into language
and matter (or Mind) into consciousness. Ideas, thus, become for us a form of cultural property, and our entre-
preneurial economies become transformed by the *presence*
of ideas. Consciousness is, by definition, a unity, a self-
naming recognition of a distinct state or condition; so consciousness becomes the primary autonomous unity. Substitute Humberto Maturana and Francisco Varela's biology of
"autopoesis and cognition"[19] for Newtonian mechanics,
and you will begin to take a few healthy steps out of our
dying industrial civilization, propped up as it is by the splin-
tering ideologies of materialism, monetarist or Marxist, and
by scientific reductionism, behavioristic or sociobiological.

The new planetary culture is not world-destroying materialism or world-denying mysticism. Contrary to the monarchical judgments of Eric Voegelin, in which philosophies not
to his taste are dismissed as "deformed,"[20] the new ecological world view is anything but "gnostic"; it is, in fact, a
loving stewardship of *this* earth. In the work of such biolo-
gists and ecologists as Lovelock, Lovins, Jackson, Margulis,
Todd, and Varela, the earth is not trashed in a seizure of
abstraction. The real latter-day gnostics are the technolo-
gists such as Marvin Minsky and Gerard O'Neill, for when
the former claims that the brain is nothing but a computer
made out of meat, and the latter that nature is an imperfect
container for culture and that only a space colony is an
appropriate vehicle for humanity, they are both revealing

the gnostic's horror of nature in a desperate wish to perfect nature through a lifting up into the state of pure technology.

In the narratives of scientific reductionism, whether the storyteller is coming out of a culture of state capitalism or scientific socialism, the individual is not important because consciousness is seen to be simply epiphenomenal to matter; therefore, consciousness can be disregarded as secondary to collective processes. It doesn't matter whether we are talking about the gene pool in sociobiology, or the communist state; the individual consciousness is not recognized to be the generatrix of value. But if $1 = 0$, then $1,000,000 \times 0 = 0$. Nothing adds up unless the value of one is seen to be the basic unity. However, if autonomy is the fundamental condition of life, and if autopoesis is the narrative process of self-description and self-performance (as it is in the biology of cognition of Maturana and Varela), then the value of the autonomous unity is fundamental to life. A failure to recognize the membrane that constitutes the living performance of the autonomous unity is to smash distinctions in an act of destruction, and whether we are speaking of sentient beings, cultures, or ecologies, this ignorant smashing of distinctions initiates an unending karmic cycle of violence, terrorism, disruption, and devastation.

If, as Gregory Bateson argued, Mind is an inseparable unity with nature, then consciousness is the production of value, and the rights of consciousness need to be protected with as much fervor as we once dedicated to the protection of the rights of property. If, on the other hand, we see Mind as epiphenomenal to matter, we will *see* information as a hunk of matter simply located in the discrete gene, exactly as E. O. Wilson does, and we will regard the individual simply as a packaging of the gene. Thus the concept of "inclusive fitness" shifts Social Darwinism from the survival of the fittest to a fitting of the survivors.[21]

If autonomy is the fundamental recognition of the distinction of life, and if autopoesis is the fundamental narrative of the process of life, then the biological politics that derive from these descriptions are radically different from sociobiology or scientific socialism. This is what I see as the Gaia Politique, a politics that is radical in the sense that it is deeply rooted *(radix)* in the understanding of life, and a politics that is truly Green and ecological and not simply the old industrial Marxist critique newly decorated with sunflowers and green paint.[22]

My generation of the seventies created a pop culture of "spacey" idealism; the generation of the eighties has created a pop culture of "grounded" realism. We had "Star Trek" and "Kung Fu"; they have "Dynasty" and "Dallas." It remains to be seen if the generation of those who will be in their thirties in the nineties will end the century with the best of both decades in a "grounded idealism." I hope so, for the last decade of the twentieth century may well be more than the end of a millennium; it may well be the last chance.

Cultural change is like morning in the Sangre de Cristo Mountains of southern Colorado: the dark shadows of the eastern range cover the entire San Louis Valley; but then the sun comes up higher, and one gets a clearer sense of the shape of the mountains, the color of light, and the play of shadows. For humanity in the old Atlantic cultural ecology, life in the new cultural ecology is intuited in a vision of shadowed dread and horror. For George Orwell, the future in which the individual was involved in a new culture of information was seen as an engulfment in the totalitarian state. The original title of *1984* was "The Last Man in Europe." Growing up in California, I have often felt like the last man *of* Europe, and my adult life has taken me back to spend more time in Europe and New York than in California; but, perhaps, because of that Pacific Shift I experienced in coming of age, I do not fear the new electronic technologies of the West or the old, irrational mysticisms of Asia. I assume that in the new mentality the Jeffersonian image of the literate citizen will be replaced by a new consciousness of our Commonlife. The human imagination need not be restricted to an eighteenth-century gentleman's notion of property and rights. In a vision of thinking full of wishes, I see this political Commonlife as something that was spiritually intuited by Saint Paul and Buddha. Without these spiritual transformations of consciousness to balance the technological changes, the new planetary culture will indeed become a real Orwellian nightmare.

Looking out over the political landscape of the United States under Reagan, I can see that we seem a long way off from a new political Enlightenment. It would appear that we are more in a period like the Renaissance than like the eighteenth century: a period of new intuitions in poetry, art, and philosophy more than a period of consolidation into political form. It all will take time, and if we lust after the end of history in visions of Leninist revolution or fundamentalist Armageddon, we will lose the reality of the present,

that point of conception in which the revolutionary incarnation is always taking place. The revolution cannot come in
time for us to quit our jobs or cancel our debts, and the end
of the world cannot come in time to eliminate the mess we
have made of history; nothing smaller than the earth is large
enough to express the revelation, and nothing smaller than
this instant is vast enough to contain all the future that we
need.

Notes

1. Jean Francois Lyotard, LA CONDITION POSTMODERNE (Paris:
    Les Editions de Minuit, 1979).

2. See "The Meta-Industrial Village" in William Irwin Thomp-
    son, DARKNESS AND SCATTERED LIGHT: FOUR TALKS ON THE
    FUTURE (New York: Doubleday, 1978).

3. Christopher Lasch in THE MINIMAL SELF (New York: Nor-
    ton, 1984) has referred to me as "a feminist fellow-traveler,"
    but on the basis of Jean Elshtain's review of my THE TIME
    FALLING BODIES TAKE TO LIGHT (THE NATION, Jan. 31,
    1981), I doubt if feminists would admit me to their company.
    My acceptance of the literature of mysticism as a valuable
    part of the fullness of human culture has consistently won the
    disfavor of the fashionable critics of the Left, from Conor
    Cruise O'Brien's distorting review of my first book to Fritz
    Raddatz's dismissal of both Robert Bly and myself as "se-
    cond-rate charlatans" whose work was not worthy of notice
    at the Forum International Conference on Mythos at Ri-
    thymnon, Crete, in April of 1984.

4. See, for example, Alain Dánelieu, SHIVA ET DIONYSOS (Paris: Fayard, 1979).

5. See Norman Myers, GAIA: AN ATLAS OF PLANET MANAGE-MENT (New York: Doubleday, 1984), to witness a textbook case of the shift from economics to ecology as the governing science and to observe just how Gaia can move from mythos to management in the Weberian routinization of charisma. I do not see this process of routinization as bad, though, undoubtedly, bad ecology will probably come out of it later.

6. Gunther Stent, THE COMING OF THE GOLDEN AGE: A VIEW OF THE END OF PROGRESS (New York: Museum of Natural History, 1969).

7. Robert Lawlor has become the voice for Schwaller de Lubicz and Alain Dánelieu in American culture. See his SACRED GEOMETRY (New York: Crossroads, 1983).

8. HESIOD'S THEOGONY, trans. Richmond Lattimore (Ann Arbor: University of Michigan Press, 1959), p. 130.

9. See William Irwin Thompson, ed., BIOLOGY AND THE WAY OF KNOWING (West Stockbridge, Mass.: Lindisfarne Press, 1986).

10. Paul Winter has printed a booklet on THE MAKING OF A MASS in the two-record album set MISSA GAIA/EARTH MASS (Litchfield, Ct.: Living Music Records).

11. Kirkpatrick Sale, "Bioregionalism: A New Way to Treat the Land," THE ECOLOGIST, vol. 14, no. 4 (1984), pp. 167–173.

12. See Norman Myers, GAIA.

13. "Thus we build real security above all when we strive to make our neighbors feel *more* secure, not less—whether on the scale of the village or the globe." Amory B. Lovins and L. Hunter Lovins, "Building a Secure Society," THE ECOLOGIST, vol. 14, no. 4 (1984), pp. 141–145.

14. H.G. Wells's film THE SHAPE OF THINGS TO COME (London: Alexander Korda, 1935) is now available in videocassette.

15. Jane Jacobs, CITIES AND THE WEALTH OF NATIONS (New York: Random, 1984).

16. See Donella Meadows, "Thinking About Planetary Resources," ANNALS OF EARTH STEWARDSHIP, vol. 2, no. 2, (1984).

17. I have tried two different approaches in imagining this new form of hieroglyphic thinking, one in nonfiction, see "The Future of Knowledge" in DARKNESS AND SCATTERED LIGHT and the other in fiction, see ISLANDS OUT OF TIME: A MEMOIR OF THE LAST DAYS OF ATLANTIS (New York: Dial Press, 1985).

18. John Locke, TWO TREATISES OF GOVERNMENT, ed. Peter Laslett (New York: New American Library, 1965), p. 330.

19. Humberto Maturana and Francisco Varela, AUTOPOESIS AND COGNITION, Boston Studies in the Philosophy of Science (Dordrecht, Holland: D. Reidl and Co., 1980), vol. 42.

20. See Eric Voegelin, Order and History, vol. 4, THE ECUMENIC AGE (Baton Rouge: Louisiana State University Press, 1974), p. 28.

21. For a more detailed discussion of my critique of E.O. Wilson's sociobiology, see chapter two of THE TIME FALLING BODIES TAKE TO LIGHT (New York: St. Martin's Press, 1981).

22. For an excellent study of the conflict between Marxism and ecology, feminism and leftist patriarchy, see Charlene Spretnak's and Fritjof Capra's GREEN POLITICS (New York: E.P. Dutton, 1984).

Index

APPENDIX

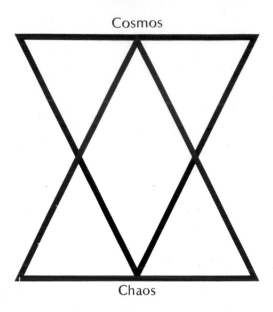

Cosmos

Chaos

FIGURE 1.
The Two Modes of Existence

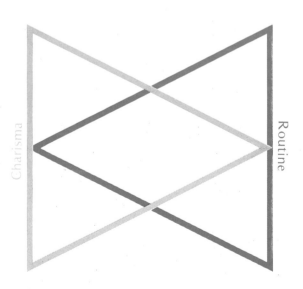

Charisma

Routine

FIGURE 2.
The Two Mediations of the Modes

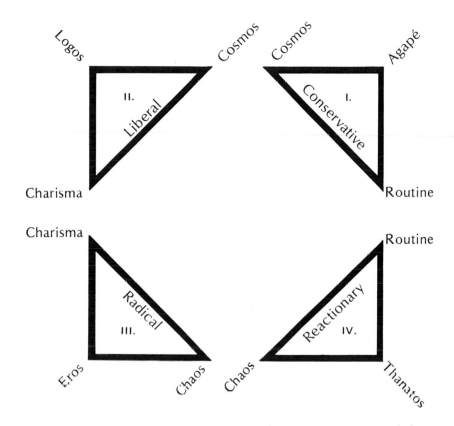

FIGURE 6.
The Four Value Orientations

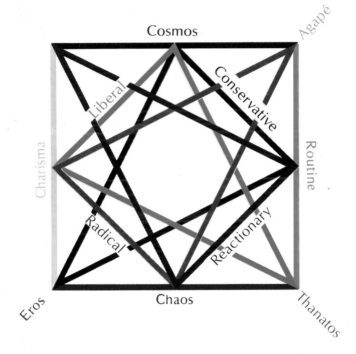

FIGURE 5.
The Four Value Orientations

    I. The Conservative
    II. The Liberal
    III. The Radical
    IV. The Reactionary

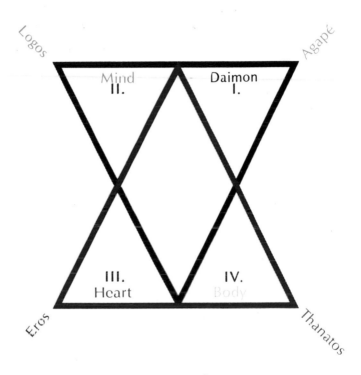

FIGURE 4.
The Four Faculties
with Their Associated Tones
of Consciousness

I. Daimon, with tone of Agapé
II. Mind, with tone of Logos
III. Heart, with tone of Eros
IV. Body, with tone of Thanatos

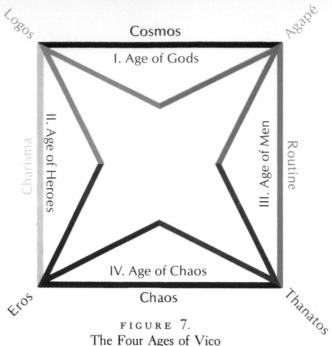

FIGURE 7.
The Four Ages of Vico

I. Age of Gods = Cosmos, Agapé, Logos
II. Age of Heroes = Charisma, Logos, Eros
III. Age of Men = Routine, Agapé, Thanatos
IV. Age of Chaos = Chaos, Eros, Thanatos

FIGURE 8.
The Figures Together:
the Two Modes, the Two Mediations, the Four Faculties and Tones,
the Four Value Orientations, and the Four Ages

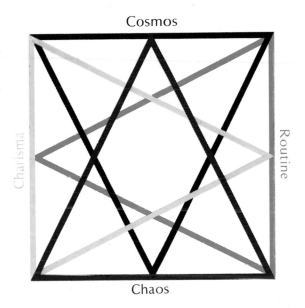

FIGURE 3.
The Basic Quaternity

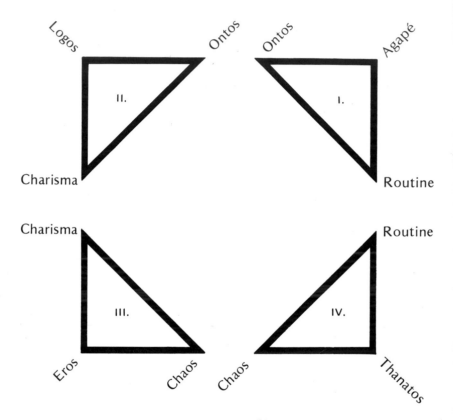

FIGURE 9.
The Four World-Economies
I. Communist
II. Capitalist
III. Developing
IV. Least Developed